FSOT Exam Prep 2020-2021

A Study Guide with 400 Test Questions and Answer Explanations for the Foreign Service Officer Test (2 Full Practice Tests)

Published by Newstone Test Prep
ISBN 978-1-989726-17-4 (paperback)

Table of Contents

Chapter 1: The U.S. Foreign Service

The U.S. Foreign Service is the main system that the U.S. Diplomatic Service uses to recruit and manage personnel. The Diplomatic Service is within the U.S. State Department, and so whatever goes on pertaining to the Foreign Service, including testing of aspiring Foreign Service Officers, falls under this department.

The Foreign Service was begun in 1924 through a law referred to as the Rogers Act, and as a single administrative unit it combines both consular and diplomatic services. This unit has authority to assign duties to diplomats working outside the U.S. The U.S. Foreign Service today has more than thirteen thousand professional employees whose responsibility it is to carry out the government's foreign policy and assist United States citizens when they are abroad.

To join the Foreign Service you must take a written exam and go through an oral assessment. Once you have passed all parts of the exam and other necessary evaluations such as the medical assessment, you can be recruited and deployed to any of 260 U.S. diplomatic missions located in different parts of the world. This includes embassies and consulates as well as different facilities used for the purposes of U.S. representation.

How the Foreign Service Operates

The U.S. Foreign Affairs function is carried out through four major agencies: the Department of State, the Department of Agriculture, the Department of Commerce and the U.S. Agency for International Development. Recruitment and deployment of Foreign Service Officers falls under the Department of State, whose headquarters are in the Harry S. Truman Building near Washington, D.C.

The director general, a presidential appointee, is charged with managing the U.S. Foreign Service. Before the director general's appointment is made official it has to be approved by the Senate first. Traditionally, this post is given to a person who has worked previously as a Foreign Service Officer. Before October 2, 2016, the director general was also the Bureau of Human Resources' director, but these positions have since been separated.

The Background of the Department of State

In order to put its current state into proper perspective it is important to understand how the Department of State historically came to be and how it has evolved. The country's first Congress passed a law in 1789 that created the Department of State. Among its important duties was to keep the Great Seal of the United States. Originally, the department had two services operating almost with autonomy: the Diplomatic Service and the Consular Service.

Whereas the Diplomatic Service had the responsibility of deploying ambassadors—referred to in the 1890s as "ministers"—to various embassies abroad, the Consular Service was responsible for assisting U.S. sailors and engaging in the promotion of international trade and general commerce.

Throughout the nineteenth century, it was solely the president who appointed ambassadors and consuls, and up until 1856 the positions were unsalaried. In those early days, the people appointed to represent the U.S. as ambassadors and consuls usually had commercial interests in the countries where they were assigned to work, and so they were expected to survive on the income they earned through private enterprise. If that was not sufficient they were expected to collect fees in their respective countries of residence. Congress made some changes in 1856, and from then on consuls began to earn salaries.

Those who qualified to earn salaries were forbidden to conduct their own businesses. However, they were allowed to continue collecting fees commensurate with the services they provided in their respective countries of residence.

The first woman appointed to serve in a senior position in the Foreign Service was in 1923, when Lucile Atcheson Curtis was appointed as a consular or diplomatic officer. In 1924, the Foreign Office consolidated the Foreign Service to make the Diplomatic and Consular functions one. This was done through the Rogers Act.

Even in those early days, people aspiring to serve in the Diplomatic Service had to pass entrance exams. These were deliberately very difficult so as to recruit only the best-performing Americans. Once recruited to work in the Diplomatic Service, the system of promotion was based solely on merit.

Through the Rogers Act, two boards were formed, one the Foreign Service and the other the Examiners of the Foreign Service. While the Foreign Service Board was charged with advising the Secretary of State on matters related to management of the Foreign Service, the Examiners of the Foreign Service Board was given the responsibility to manage the relevant exam process.

Representatives of the Department of Commerce abroad were accorded diplomatic status through legislation passed by Congress in 1927, forming the Foreign Commerce service. Up to that point in time these representatives were referred to as "trade commissioners."

In 1930 Congress passed a law transforming the U.S. Department of Agriculture into the U.S. Foreign Agricultural Service. Although the department already had diplomatic status, its employees—commercial as well as agricultural attachés—remained civil servants, meaning they were not considered Foreign Service Officers.

These attachés were reassigned to the Department of State in 1939. In 1954 Congressional legislation returned the agricultural attachés to their former department, the Department of Agriculture. As for the commercial attachés, their position remained unchanged until the Foreign Service Act of 1980 was enacted.

Employment as per the Foreign Service Act of 1946

The Department of State requested the creation of classes for categorizing employees, and Congress passed a law to that effect in 1946, creating six classes: Foreign Service Officers and chiefs of mission; Foreign Service staff and Foreign Service reservists; alien personnel, subsequently referred to as foreign and local service nationals; and consular agents.

The expectation was that these officers were going to spend most of their working life abroad, so they were commissioned as U.S. officers ready to offer service anywhere in the world. Nevertheless, reserve officers normally spent most of their working life within Washington, DC.

The personnel that comprised the Foreign Service Staff included support staff and people who held clerical positions. There was an intention to dismantle any distinction that existed between the staff of the Foreign Service and Civil Service, because the distinction generated some friction. Through the 1946 Foreign Service Act, the 1927 and 1930 acts that granted representatives of the USDA diplomatic status were rendered redundant and repealed. It was necessary to repeal those laws because by that time the affected representatives or attachés had already been put under the Department of State that was responsible for their appointment in the first place.

It was also the 1946 act that replaced the Board of Foreign Service Personnel with the Board of the Foreign Service and created the position of director general of the Foreign Service. The new board had a broader mandate besides managing the personnel system.

A system was developed where if an officer failed to earn promotions over a specified time period, there would be no option but to require his or her retirement. This concept, dubbed a system of 'up-or-out,' was borrowed from the United States Navy. The 1946 acts also created the career minister position. Only senior officers were given the title. Finally, this act set the compulsory age for retirement for staff serving in the Foreign Service.

Employment as per the Foreign Service Act of 1980

Although the amendments made in the act of 1946 introduced some good initial changes, further changes were adopted during the 1970s. In preparation for drafting the 1980 act, Congress recommended the return of all commercial attachés to the Department of Commerce, while retaining their Foreign Service Officer status. Others included in the department were agricultural attachés, FSOs in the State Department, U.S. Information Agency and United States Agency for International Development (USAID).

This act scrapped the category of Foreign Officers named the Foreign Service Reserve. At the same time, the non-diplomatic personnel system that engaged staff locally for staff working abroad was reformed. The Senior Foreign Service was created, comprising a ranking structure resembling the one used in the armed forces, and even the Senior Executive Service.

In addition, the act introduced remuneration termed 'danger pay' meant for U.S. Diplomats serving in areas considered dangerous or hostile.

Fresh authority was also given to the Board of Foreign Service, which was required to include at least one representative from a range of departments and offices, among them the State Department; the U.S. Information Agency and USAID; Agriculture, Commerce and Labor Departments; Office of Personnel Management and Office of Management & Budget; the Equal Employment Opportunity Commission and any additional agency the U.S. President decided to designate. The board was also chosen as advisor to the State Secretary with regards to issues related to the Foreign Service.

Important Members of the Foreign Service

Members of the U.S. Foreign Service are well defined by law.

Chief of Mission
Chiefs of mission in the U.S. are presidential appointees, although the president must obtain Senate approval with regard to appointments. The chief of mission (COM), or head of mission (HOM), serves as an ambassador or high commissioner, permanent representative, consul-general or nuncio or charge d'affaires as the situation requires.

Officials heading representative offices of some international organizations are sometimes also referred to as mission heads. In the meantime, the officials deputizing the heads of missions are given the title of deputy chief of mission (DCM). Where ambassadors are political appointees without career pre-qualifications, which means they are not necessarily career diplomats, the most senior Foreign Service professional is the deputy chief of mission.

There are also some professionals heading international bodies' offices who are neither heads nor deputies of missions, but they are nevertheless the most senior officials in the respective countries they are based in. A good example is a project manager of an international organization. Such senior personnel are referred to as "Chiefs of Staff," and this title should not be confused with "Chiefs of Mission."

Ambassadors at Large in General

Ambassadors at large are appointees of the president and require Senate confirmation.

A person holding this position can be a diplomat or a secretary, or even a high-ranking minister accredited to be a representative of the country he or she comes from and its people at the international level. An ambassador at large is different from an ambassador in residence in that the latter is normally restricted to one country or one embassy, whereas the former is given the mandate to work in different countries, mostly neighboring one another. The operations of an ambassador at large can even cover an entire region, and sometimes such an official has a seat at international bodies such as the UN or the European Union.

There are even cases where the state or government takes advice from the ambassador at large. Such deployments have historically been made by heads of states, where for instance a prime minister or president designates a special diplomatic envoy for a specific assignment abroad. Other times an ambassador at large is assigned to delve into a specific issue in the home country.

Whether one is an ambassador in the traditional sense or an ambassador at large, international protocol dictates that they are referred to as His or Her Excellency or Mr. or Madam Ambassador. These titles are abbreviated as "H.E."

Ambassadors at Large in the U.S.

In the United States, the first ambassador at large was appointed by the president in March 1949, after invoking Article II, Section 2 of the United States Constitution. Within the State Department's Diplomatic Corps, the positions of ambassadors at large include coordinator for counterterrorism; ambassador at large for issues of war crimes; ambassador at large for global women's issues; ambassador at large to monitor and combat human trafficking; United States global AIDS coordinator; and ambassador at large for international religious freedom.

Senior Foreign Service Members (SFS)

Members of the Senior Foreign Service (SFS) in the U.S. are senior leaders and experts in the management of the Foreign Service. They are also presidential appointees, as approved by the Senate. SFSs can come from the ranks of Foreign Service Officers or specialists.

The top four U.S. Foreign Service ranks were formulated by the Foreign Service Act of 1980 as well as Executive Order 12293. These ranks were designed to give the Foreign Service senior grades that correspond to those in the military as well as the navy, assigning ranks to individuals and not to specific positions.

For example, where in the military ranks range from 0 to 10, in the SFS rankings a person is a career ambassador (FE – CA). Military rank 0 – 9 corresponds to the SFS rank of career minister (FE – CM) while military rank 0 – 8 corresponds to the SFS rank of minister counselor (FE – MC). Military rank 0 – 7 corresponds to the SFS rank of counselor (FE – OC).

The 1980 Foreign Service Act stipulates that the U.S. president may confer the rank of career ambassador upon a member of the Senior Foreign Service who is a career officer, recognizing his or her exemplary service spanning a reasonable period of time. The act also allows the president to set the salary categories for officers in the Senior Foreign Service and give suitable titles to those classes.

The three remaining SFS senior positions were created by President Reagan by Executive Order 12293. Career ambassadors are supposed to be addressed as "The Honorable" and not His or Her Excellency.

A Little History of the U.S. Foreign Service

Before the 1980 Foreign Service Act was passed, there was a grading system for the Foreign Service Officers established by the Rogers Act and later by the 1946 Foreign Service Act. That grading system ranged from FSS-22 to FSO-1. Within this system was one 'senior' grade, the career minister, a position established by the act of 1946. This senior grade was intended for FSOs known to have served with distinction within the position of ambassador or other similar positions such as assistant secretary or under secretary of state.

In those days, career ministers had salaries equal to any senior FSO-1, so their promotion was essentially symbolic.

The Career Ambassador's Rank

The rank of career ambassador was established in 1955 and was intended to amend the 1946 act. It gave the U.S. president certain powers and guidelines relating to promotion of FSOs. After obtaining Senate approval, the president was mandated to appoint a person to the post of career ambassador to individuals who had served 15 years in a senior position within a government agency. Within those 15 years, an individual must also have served a minimum of three years as a U.S. career minister and have fulfilled all state secretary requirements. Furthermore, the person must have rendered service to the government in an outstandingly distinguished manner.

As a matter of regulation, all ambassadors were appointed only from the FSO-2 rank to the FSO-1 rank, and the utmost senior positions were given to career ministers, who were actually rare, and to career ambassadors, who were even rarer. After the U.S. Civil Service was reformed in 1949, the General Schedule that had just three "super grades" that run from GS-16 to GS-18 was put in place. In 1978 the Senior Executive Service was created and in the process, senior FSOs who handled policy matters were oddly positioned equal to mid-level officers in the military and the civil service. This unfortunate imbalance was partially sorted out through the act of 1980, as discussed earlier.

Reason Behind the Creation of the Senior FSO Position

The creation of the senior position within the Foreign Service in 1980 was intended to put in place a cadre comprising Foreign Affairs professionals at the senior level who had positions that corresponded with senior officers within the military and navy. These positions also corresponded to the Senior Executive Service within the civil service that had been put in place only a couple of years earlier.

The 1980 act stipulates that in order for an individual to qualify to become an ambassador, among other conditions, an SFS officer must have served at a senior level in a United States diplomatic mission, such as deputy chief of mission, section head at a big embassy or consul general. Such an officer must, according to the 1980 act, have served at the headquarters in the same capacity he or she held at agencies of the Foreign Affairs.

Chapter 2: How Best to Select a Career Track

While it is a feat to pass the FSOT, you need to learn more about the choices you have when it comes to narrowing down your specialization. A successful FSO candidate is expected to select a preferred career track from the five available in the Foreign Service. During the testing process, specifically during the QEP assessment, the panel normally narrows specific questions down to your chosen career track so it can see how well suited you are to the task. To help you make an informed choice, this book provides you with information regarding each of the five FSO career tracks.

Career as a Management Officer

To become a management officer you will have qualified to work as a Foreign Service Officer, but you will now be involved mainly in matters pertaining to business management. Management officers are based at the embassy, where they have their own office, referred to as the management office. They are not expected to share an office with the ambassador, who is the topmost ranking government representative in a foreign country.

Where the government has no embassy but has established a consulate, a management officer in the FSO is put in charge. A consulate—the location of a government's representation in a foreign country—is of a lower rank than an embassy. Where the government establishes a consulate in place of an embassy, no officer is deployed in the country as an ambassador.

Unfortunately, sometimes consulates take longer to deliver services because there are instances where they need to forward people's requests to their nearest embassy for processing. Take the example of Australia, which has a consulate in San Francisco. Processing of passports might take a little longer than anticipated because the consulate does not offer that service. Instead, they forward the requests they receive for issuance or renewal of passports to the Australian embassy in Washington, DC.

As a management officer, you are expected to be resourceful, creative and quick-thinking. You also need to be action-oriented and a problem-solver, as you are the officer who staff and other people will reach out to with regards to operations at the embassy.

It is important to note that as a management officer you are not restricted to routine office work but will instead engage in roles that require high-level critical thinking skills. In fact, you should expect to be the person receiving most of the challenging questions at the embassy or consulate. Management officers who employ skillful diplomacy in order to solve problems have a great chance of advancing to ambassador positions where diplomatic skills are highly valued.

Management officers must develop solutions that are efficient and on point in a fast-paced, complex environment. Many of the issues management officers deal with are cross-disciplinary including real estate, taxation, social security, budgeting and playing a major role when new embassies or consulates are being built or established.

Another task is the coordination of different U.S. agencies so that they can work cohesively together in advancing the functions of the Foreign Service. Management officers coordinate visits by senior government officials and interact with them when they arrive. Furthermore, management officers promote professional development opportunities for members of the Foreign Service.

Management officers look after the safety of Foreign Service personnel and American civilians in foreign countries and ensure any assets and installations belonging to the United States are well secured.

Career Track of a Management Officer

An FSO has great room for advancement. In fact, officers are advised to look forward to advancing up the career ladder. A management officer has straightforward steps for advancement and has the potential to become an ambassador.

Management Officer Entry Level

As a new employee at the Foreign Office, a management officer is expected to run a unit right within the embassy's management section. There is also a chance of being the only management officer in the Foreign Office if the U.S. post in that country is small.

Whether you're working in a small office in a consulate or a big office in a big embassy, you need to be a good planner and problem-solver. In short, people visiting the office should be able to feel they have been appropriately attended to. Moreover, the staff at the embassy or at smaller U.S. posts where you work, including the ambassador, should be able to depend on you to solve their problems, both work-related and sometimes concerning their families.

Management officers are expected to keep a wide range of contacts within the country where they are posted including people active in business and different officials. It is expected that management officers will strive to learn foreign languages that come in handy in the course of duty. At the entry level, a management officer's skills in negotiating are tested, and you need to learn the methods that do and do not work in your host country, especially with respect to the local culture.

To improve your prospects of promotion and advancement, you need to be able to supervise a bigger number of employees than your colleagues within the management officer track, and be able to resolve issues of an administrative nature with autonomy.

Management Officer Mid-Level

As a mid-level management officer, you should be able to run an entire management section. The same case applies if you are working at a consulate. You also should have the capacity to supervise the human resources unit or any other major unit at your embassy or consulate. You must also be able to develop and manage a budget whose size runs into millions of dollars.

You are expected to be able to manage leases and oversee the maintenance of residences owned by the government on short-term leases and buildings housing embassy offices. You will provide a platform for logistical support for the high-level visits that may occur from time to time. As a mid-level management officer, you should be able to negotiate with the authorities of your host government in matters relating to diplomatic privileges as well as immunity. Other issues you are expected to handle include laws pertaining to tax reciprocity and employment of a member of an FSO's family.

Management Officer Senior Level

Once you have reached the management officer senior level as an FSO, you can be appointed the country's deputy chief of mission or ambassador. Or you could be made a principal officer at a big consulate, or a management counselor within one of the country's large posts.

If, by the time you reach the level of senior management, you're working in Washington, DC, you could be made an office director or an executive director. There is also a chance you could be made a deputy assistant secretary, whose role is to direct resources meant to be used in support of the work carried out within the U.S. posts in various parts of the region. At this level you may be entrusted with management of global logistics for the department and for developing different programs. Other roles you are expected to be able to handle include coordinating the training of FSO staff and overseeing various assignments carried out by Foreign Service personnel.

Career as a Consular Officer

As a consular officer you should expect to work in a U.S. embassy adjudicating visas and helping U.S. citizens in times of emergency. You can also expect to serve as the primary embassy contact with people who need the services of the embassy or the consulate. Then, as you become more conversant with the work of a consular officer you may be entrusted with managing some sections of the embassy, eventually being entrusted to head an office.

Another important task you may find yourself handling is facilitation of adoption, which is a responsibility under the docket of consular officers. You'll be required to assist in evacuating Americans as needed and reunifying them afterward. Other responsibilities may include fighting fraud, overseeing border protection and working to stop human trafficking. Essentially, the work of consular officers helps them make a big impact in people's personal lives. Critically, consular officers reassure families that have been caught up in a crisis.

As a consular officer, you should be able to engage in strategic thinking. You are the officer charged with managing crises and protecting any citizens of the U.S. in your host country even as you protect U.S. assets in the foreign land. You are expected as a consular officer to employ your problem-solving skills as well as your managerial skills to surmount any challenges Americans may encounter in their travels or when living abroad, or even in the course of conducting business in the country. This explanation should suffice to disabuse you of the notion that the main work of consular and management officers is to stamp passports and issue visas.

Consular officers are entrusted with making sound judgments pertaining to foreign nationals wishing to travel to America. You may also end up handling a wide range of challenges like child custody disputes, arrests of U.S. nationals and travel advisories. Consular officers are charged with paying visits to any U.S. citizens arrested in the host country, and ensuring they get access to legal representation. You'll work closely with the host country's officials in a bid to enhance legitimate businesses, boost education and make travel for tourists easier.

A consular officer is expected to acquire expertise pertaining to the laws, culture, economy and politics of the host country. That expertise should then be used to make timely decisions that can affect U.S. citizens' lives both in the host country and also back in the U.S. Consular officers should be ready to lead a staff of highly qualified members from diverse cultural backgrounds.

Career Track of a Consular Officer

Next you will see how a consular officer progresses from the lowest rank to the highest—the consular officer career track.

Consular Officer Entry Level

As a new employee in the position of consular officer, you should expect to have a number of employees under you, so you need to have supervisory skills. Many of these employees will have been hired locally in your host country. You will also be expected to perform adjudication of visas. Another one of your roles is to help U.S. nationals who are residing abroad or paying short visits to the country and who may be caught up in an emergency such as arrests and hospitalizations. Your role also includes facilitating birth certificates, processing of passport applications and providing notary services.

An entry-level consular officer is expected to provide responses to inquiries made to the embassy or consulate by attorneys, representatives in Congress, different government officials and business people. In addition you are expected to combat any fraud you may notice in the course of performing your consular duties.

Consular Officer Mid-Level

At the mid-level, a consular officer is expected to be able to handle management of a midsized consular section. For example, as a mid-level consular officer you may be assigned to oversee the American Citizen Services (ACS), the anti-fraud unit or the embassy unit dealing with visas.

You may also be charged with supervising entry-level American officers, as well as the locally engaged staff (LES). You must be able to make complex decisions pertaining to visa issuance and services to U.S. citizens. You should also be able to resolve challenging issues related to human resources and workflow. If you are deployed to Washington, DC, you are expected to provide support to the consular officers there in matters associated with visas and ACS, as well as issues with fraud and management.

Consular Officer Senior Level

Having reached the senior level as a consular officer within the FSO, you may be entrusted with managing an entire consular section and supervising a reasonable number of American officers as well as LES. At this level you are considered part of the U.S. embassy's senior management.

You qualify at this level to become an office director, and you can be deployed to Washington, DC, particularly in the Bureau for Consular Affairs. You will be involved in different outreach functions including addressing the press and speaking to different organizations in the U.S.

At this peak of your career, you can be considered for the post of deputy chief of mission, ambassador or even principal officer in a big American consulate.

Career as an Economic Officer

As an economic officer, you should anticipate engaging in treaty negotiations and networking with the host country, as well as varying developments of an economic nature. In short, as a newly employed economic officer you should expect to be involved in economic matters directly affecting the people of your host country, whereas senior officials within your career track will focus on development of U.S. policy associated with economic and trade issues.

Economic officers are known to work closely with governments of foreign countries as well as different agencies of the U.S. government in matters pertaining to technology and science, energy and trade and issues of an economic and/or environmental nature. Economic officers address matters that affect both their host countries and the U.S. itself.

Economic officers are considered very resourceful negotiators, and they are expected to build and enhance relations in trade and other economic activities between the United States and foreign countries. While promoting national security through enhancement of economic activity they are expected to work closely with the government of the United States, government officials from foreign countries, leaders in the business sector, international bodies and people known to influence public opinion.

One misconception many people have regarding the economic officer track within the Foreign Service is that you must be very knowledgeable in quantitative economics to do well. Such deep knowledge is not necessary, although having a background in economics can help. The main focus of economic officers at the Foreign Office is actually on developing relationships with important personalities in a host country's business sector and other people who are important in matters of the economy. They are also expected to develop relationships with the government as well as the opposition, NGOs, academia and multilateral bodies.

Economic officers in the Foreign Service have a very important responsibility because what they report about the economic trends and prevailing conditions in their host countries may influence U.S. government policy. They liaise with economic organizations of international standards and other governments in resolving challenges affecting marketing, promoting fair practices and advocating for United States policy. It is also an economic officer's responsibility to liaise with other foreign countries in addressing science, environmental issues and matters of health.

Economic officers are expected to identify opportunities for American businesses at a global level, and also should make sure U.S. enterprises are allowed to compete fairly when investing and trading abroad. They are expected to work towards reducing any economic impediments and to promote economic development in underdeveloped or emerging countries. They negotiate agreements and promote policies meant to enhance safety and security as well as efficiency in travel and goods transportation.

These officers research and analyze the implications of the global energy supply on United States' interests wherever they are. Promoting communications' technology development and infrastructure is another duty.

Career Track of an Economic Officer

Very importantly, economic officers are expected to engage in building and maintaining positive economic and trade relations between foreign countries and the U.S. At the end of the day, it is this competence and others already mentioned that help an economic officer to quickly climb the career ladder. Next you will see what the career track of an economic officer looks like.

Economic Officer Entry Level

When you have been freshly recruited in the Foreign Service under the economic track, you should anticipate working within a section dealing with economic matters, under the supervision and direction of an experienced economic officer. Your job will most likely be to develop a good network of contacts within your host government, which includes the business community. This network is meant to keep you informed of the goings-on in the local scene. Another of your responsibilities as an economic officer just starting your career is preparing economic analyses as required, and making policy recommendations for the U.S. to consider.

If you are deployed to a small U.S. post, another of your responsibilities could be supervising a few local employees hired to work on issues of trade and managing a small library.

Economic Officer Mid-Level

At this level you are expected to operate as a head or chief of a midsized economic affairs office. You will be specifically charged with supervising LES in addition to newly employed entry-level economic officers.

It is also your responsibility at this level to brief your ambassador and any visiting U.S. dignitaries or business people regarding local conditions and U.S. policy. You must also provide support as needed during their visit.

You are expected to either personally provide an economic report for Washington, DC, or have someone create the economic report while you supervise. With guidance from your seniors, you may be asked to persuade your host government to provide support for U.S. policies pertaining to different economic, environmental and commercial issues.

Economic Officer Senior Level

As a senior level economic officer, you will take charge of the development and implementation of U.S. policy regarding bilateral and multilateral trade as well as other economic issues. This is inclusive of matters touching on possible debt relief, free trade and international finance and providing developmental aid.

If you are deployed to Washington, DC, you will likely travel as the United States' government negotiator in bilateral and multilateral treaties, especially pertaining to issues to do with aviation, the environment and investment. It is important to note that as a senior economic officer in the Foreign Service you stand a good chance of rising to the office of director, where you will be expected to supervise a large number of Foreign Service Officers. You will also be in charge of a large economic or political and economic section, whereby you will be expected to advise the ambassador on a wide range of issues of economic importance.

At this top level, you will be required to make demarches to the government hosting you, and you should be prepared to meet with government officials including the minister of finance, minister of trade and others dealing with the economy, communication, transport, the environment and labor. Other officials you will be expected to meet with as appropriate include those from the host country's Central Bank, Civil Aviation Authority and Chamber of Commerce.

Career as a Political Officer

As a political officer in the Foreign Service, you are expected to work closely with the local community, and for that reason you need to have a clear understanding of the local culture. You particularly need to understand the people and the main languages they use. Another of your responsibilities is to monitor politics as they unfold on the local scene, and to work with respected political personalities in conveying the U.S. political point of view. Officers holding senior positions in the Foreign Office are expected to help in the management and supervision of lower-level political officers, whether in the U.S. or in a foreign country.

It is also the duty of political officers to thoroughly analyze host countries' political happenings, and to engage in necessary negotiations and effective communications with foreign government officials at every level. Political officers are considered informed and knowledgeable negotiators who are adept at interpreting situations and providing appropriate advice regarding matters of international importance.

Political officers are expected to have a trained eye focused on the country's political climate. It is assumed they are capable of deciphering events of a political nature as they unfold so that they can predict a likely outcome with regards to U.S. interests in the country. As a political officer, you are also expected to be able to negotiate with foresight, and to link happenings with relevant policies already in place.

There is often a misconception that to become an ambassador you have to first be a political officer. This is incorrect. Of course, there are political officers who end up becoming ambassadors, but the two are not mutually exclusive.

As a political officer you will need to have outstanding communication skills. You'll be regularly communicating with representatives of foreign governments when seeking support for goals the U.S. shares with those governments. Your communication skills will also come in handy when seeking votes in a multinational forum.

Other responsibilities given to political officers in the Foreign Office include development of contacts in foreign countries within and without of government and the political arena. These are contacts you can use to advance the political interests of the U.S. government.

As a political officer you should be able to assess the impact of any political development in your host country on the United States, and make appropriate recommendations as to how the U.S. government should respond. It is also your responsibility to support visits of high-level personalities and to advise policy makers on the best way to carry out communication with foreign governments. You should monitor activities being carried out by international bodies which the U.S. does not belong to such as the European Union and other groups of significance.

As you have already seen, as a political officer in the Foreign Service you will be expected to engage in negotiations where you should interpret the politics of your host country appropriately and provide suitable advice, and also take what you understand about the country's politics and communicate it to the U.S. government while offering your best advice regarding the situation. You are also expected to do the same in other matters of international importance. In short, yours is expected to be a trained eye when it comes to your host country's political atmosphere in relation to the interests of the United States.

Career Track of a Political Officer

A political officer begins at the bottom of the ladder immediately after joining the Foreign Service, but there is room, just like in other career tracks in the Foreign Service, to rise to the highest level, including the potential to become an ambassador.

Political Officer Entry Level

When you are newly employed as a political officer in the Foreign Service, you are entrusted with reporting on a single segment of the local society, such as a religious sector, a particular geographic area and so on. You are also expected to establish contacts with local leaders as well as different officials at various levels in government as well as within political parties with clout.

You can be assigned to oversee the work of a political specialist engaged locally for his or her contacts at high levels of society.

At this level you are required to regularly read locally published newspapers and magazines and to accompany senior level officers as needed. When you are in the company of senior officials, you are expected to take notes and to subsequently report on meetings.

Political Officer Mid-Level

Once you have reached mid-level as a political officer in the Foreign Service, you are deemed fit to offer your services as head of a midsized section pertaining to politics or matters of a political-economic nature. You are expected to keep in contact with prominent figures in the political arena, the labor industry, within the military and different other sectors both in and out of government.

You can now also be entrusted with supervising entry-level political officers and political experts hired from the host country. Another responsibility you can anticipate at this level is monitoring and analyzing important issues and reporting on them accordingly. You are also deemed skilled enough to spearhead demarches to the government of your host country and to clearly explain the United States' position to different diplomats. It is expected that you will gather useful information from the individuals you engage with.

It is also your responsibility to supervise scheduling during visits made by officials from Washington, DC, ensuring those schedules are in line with U.S. foreign policy objectives. You should make a point of accompanying U.S. visitors on their local visits so that you can take notes as they engage with local officials or other key public personalities.

At this level you are qualified to represent the interests of the United States at gatherings of international organizations. You will be expected to carry out coordination of all responses to various issues discussed and to liaise with the organizations' staff as necessary. Whenever there are high-level meetings held, it's your responsibility to ensure sufficient information is procured in a timely fashion to the delegates from Washington, DC.

Political Officer Senior Level

At the senior level as a political officer in the Foreign Service, you are deemed ready to handle management of a section within an embassy, which deals with matters of a political or political-economic nature. You are also ready to supervise lower-level political officers and will be relied upon to provide appropriate advice to the ambassador and to send demarches to your host government.

Political officers of this cadre are expected to meet on a regular basis with different political and community leaders, and to sometimes speak in public, if deemed helpful, to explain the position of the United States on certain issues of importance. This aspect of giving speeches is particularly likely when you serve from Washington, DC.

You may be given an office to direct or be assigned an advisory role to your senior at the department. You can also be charged with heading delegations when there are meetings held abroad, whether bilateral or multilateral in nature. You could also be entrusted with drafting policy documents as well as statements on behalf of senior officials at the department, which are meant to be used by various foreign embassies.

Career as a Public Diplomacy Officer

In plain terms, a public diplomacy officer is an information officer. This is an officer in the Foreign Service whose main role is influencing public opinion toward United States' interests. You should expect to work with the media in your host country and personalities in cultural leadership, and others you view as beneficial to your role. Eventually, you should be able to manage programs of importance all over the country, where your aim will be to disseminate information pertaining to democracy and free speech.

As a public diplomacy officer, you should anticipate engaging with opinion leaders and local NGOs, as well as upcoming leaders. You should also be prepared to engage with academics and think tanks, as well as officials from your host government. As you engage all these people, your aim should be to inform them of US policy goals and to engage their cooperation in achieving these.

As a public diplomacy officer you are expected to be good at communication and well versed in cross-cultural associations so that you are able to enhance public awareness and be successful in promoting the Unites States' interests in foreign countries. This will involve both traditional media such as television and also radio, social media, newspapers, etc.

The information provided in this section of the book is very useful as some people imagine public diplomacy as a career that only engages with the media and cultural activities and not much else. But as you have seen, FSOs have an important role to play in advancing the agenda of the United States abroad.

In addition to maintaining numerous contacts with important people in the host country and influencing public opinion, public diplomacy officers also manage people and programs, as well as budgets and important resources. One of your tasks will be to explain to audiences in your host country how U.S. history and its values and traditions have shaped the country's foreign policy. You should be able to create and manage programs of a cultural nature and others that are purely informative to try and connect with the local people.

You will be expected to coordinate exchange programs meant to strengthen existing relationships between the U.S. and foreign countries. Such programs improve the impression foreigners have of American society, and help to enhance understanding between the U.S. and different countries.

Career Track of a Public Diplomacy Officer

Public diplomacy officers strengthen diplomatic ties between the U.S. and other countries. They play a key role in enhancing the United States' reputation overseas. Next you will see how a public diplomacy officer in the Foreign Service climbs the career ladder.

Public Diplomacy Officer, Entry Level

At the entry level as a public diplomacy officer in the Foreign Service, you should expect to play an assistant role to the Foreign Office's cultural affairs officer, or the information officer. You may also be charged with coordinating exchange programs. Or you could be tasked with overseeing the consular website and making use of varied technologies in support of the Foreign Service function.

You might be called upon to serve on the board that monitors the Fulbright selection in your host country, and to monitor travel programs and professional programs of the grantees locally and in the U.S. You will be the contact person for both local and foreign reporters. The media will contact you when it needs accurate information from the embassy or consulate pertaining to the U.S.' stance on a particular issue or policy. You will promote free speech and the United States' core values.

Public Diplomacy Officer Mid-Level

As a more skilled public diplomacy officer, having reached the middle level in your career track, you may be entrusted with managing staff working in the embassy's cultural or information section. You could also be charged with overseeing the budget for exchange programs. At this stage in your career you will be deemed capable of organizing focus programs as well as discussion forums or groups comprising local people, where topics of mutual interest to your host country and the U.S. can be discussed.

You may be asked to take charge of the management of the embassy's information resource center or its language institute. At this stage in your career, you qualify to sit on the Fulbright board or might even chair the Fulbright commission.

Public Diplomacy Officer Senior Level

As a senior level public diplomacy officer in Foreign Service, you are expected to be competent enough to manage exchange programs in Washington, DC, at the regional and global level. You are a representative of the U.S. government at one of its embassies abroad, serving as the government's spokesperson and the officer responsible for managing cultural and media programs. You will handle large budgets and manage resources associated with staff.

Your job will also be to advise your ambassador and senior colleagues at the Foreign Service of matters associated with the media, and to furnish them with information of a cultural nature and/or pertaining to education in your host country.

Chapter 3: What You Need to Know About the FSOT

The Foreign Service Officer Test (FSOT) helps determine if a person is well prepared to join the U.S. government service as a Foreign Service Officer or FSO. The FSOT covers a range of topics that include the use of the English language, knowledge of the Foreign Service Officer job and information on important biographies. The exam also includes an essay.

Who is Eligible to Become an FSO?

• You must be a citizen of the U.S.

• You must be between the ages of 20 and 59

• You must be at least 21 when appointed an FSO, but not older than 60

• You must be available to serve worldwide and/or in Washington, DC

How Registration for the FSOT is Done

At least five weeks prior to taking the exam, candidates must submit an application and select a seat at a testing facility. The latter ensures there is no hassle at the testing center on exam day.

Once you register, your application is only valid for the particular test for which you have registered, so when that particular testing window closes, your registration for the FSOT becomes invalid and you can't use it to take the test during a different testing window. Three days before the testing window opens, registration closes.

If you require accommodation and there is documentation warranting it, you need to submit your request and ensure it is received for approval before the date the FSOT is scheduled to take place. Also note that once you have submitted your application to take the FSOT during a particular testing window, you can't change it. You also can't take the test more than once in a 12-month period.

Regularity of FSOT

You can register and take the FSOT in any of the three open periods, which are February, June and October.

Fees Charged for the FSOT

A $5 fee is charged, but it's refunded in full within three weeks of your taking the test. This refund does not apply to candidates who do not show up for the test or fail to make a formal cancelation at least 48 hours before the scheduled test time. Instead, such candidates are charged a $72 no-show fee.

How Many Times Can You Try the FSOT?

You can register and take the FSOT as many times as you want as long as you fulfill the conditions already mentioned and wait for 12 months in between registrations. For instance, if you take the FSOT in October 2019, the first time you are eligible to retest is October 2020, and if you try to register before then your registration will be rejected.

How Long Do You Have to Wait after Canceling?

If you cancel a scheduled test for which you had successfully registered you can register again without having to wait 12 months.

Are You Allowed to Change Your Career Track?

Yes, you can change your career track during the five-week registration period.

Can You Take the FSOT Outside the U.S.?

Yes, you can take the FSOT in centers outside the U.S. The FSOT is also administered outside the country at Pearson VUE Professional Centers (PPCs). These centers, which are always outside capital cities, are neither owned nor run by the government but are Pearson VUE facilities. For identification purposes, you will be required to show your U.S. passport.

FSOT Centers Outside the U.S.

You can find test centers outside the U.S. in the following places:

American Samoa – Pago Pago

Australia – Melbourne and Sydney

Brazil – Sao Paolo

Canada – Edmonton, Montreal, Ottawa, Vancouver and Toronto.

France – Paris

Germany – Frankfurt

Greece – Athens

Guam – Tamuning

Japan – Osaka and Tokyo

Mexico – Mexico City

Northern Mariana Islands – Saipan

Puerto Rico – Guaynabo

Singapore – Singapore City

South Africa – Johannesburg

South Korea – Seoul

South Sudan – Juba

Spain – Madrid

Taiwan – Taipei

Thailand – Bangkok

Turkey – Istanbul

UK – London

Anytime you want to find the embassies or consulates with upcoming FSOT tests you can log on to careers.state.gov/work/foreign-service/officer/test-process. Do this around four days before the registration window opens and you will find a list of places offering the test. Be aware that all of the U.S. embassies in the places mentioned have the discretion to offer or not offer the FSOT during any of the testing windows depending on availability of resources.

Availability of On-Base Test Centers

On-base test centers (OBTC) also exist. These are located within U.S. military facilities both within and without the U.S. Candidates taking their test from such centers have extra options for test appointments whenever a testing window opens, but such candidates should still contact their target center ahead of time regarding test taking. Once you have submitted your application, you will be able to access a user-friendly database to view all the sites where FSOT testing is available.

Is it Possible to Amend an Application?

Once you have submitted your application for FSOT registration, you can't access it to amend it, even if you're having second thoughts about the career track you chose. Once you submit your application for a particular testing cycle, it's done and you'll have to wait for another testing window to re-register and change any information including career track. If the five-week registration period is not over yet and you would like to alter or cancel your appointment, you can do that. But only under extraordinary circumstances can you change your appointment after the five-week registration period has lapsed, and you'll need to supply documentation for why you couldn't make your original appointment.

What to do if Your Center is not Listed

If you don't see your center when you click the drop-down box during registration, choose "Other" and then "Other Domestic."

How Long Does the FSOT Take?

Normally the FSOT takes three hours, but sometimes that time is extended to three and a half hours to allow for extra questions that are added solely for the sake of research. Such additional questions, though not identified on the test, are not included in the scoring.

FSOT Results

You can expect your FSOT results around two weeks after the testing window closes. If you don't receive an email with your results during the anticipated time, check your spam folder. This is important because your results will tell you the day you're scheduled for the next part of the assessment, discussing your Personal Narrative. This date can't be rescheduled and there are no exceptions. Not even technical glitches are considered.

What to Do if You're Not Satisfied With Your Score

It is unlikely the computer-based multiple-choice section of the test will have scoring errors, so there is no provision for rescoring. In short, you have to accept your score on that part of the test. The essay can be reassessed if you make the request and pay a fee of $30, which should be done within 45 days of the scores being released.

Note that rescoring your FSOT score doesn't guarantee a higher score. However, if it does and your score reaches a '6,' your status will be altered to reflect a pass for the essay. You will then be moved to the category of candidates eligible for the Personal Narrative & QEP.

There is also a chance your new score could be lower than what you were accorded before the reassessment. If that happens and the score drops below '6,' your status will be altered so you're placed in the category of candidates who didn't pass the exam and can't move forward with the next steps of the testing process. In short, if your essay is reassessed, the second score is taken to be the final one. After your essay has been reassessed, you should expect to receive your new results within two or three weeks. Note that copies of candidates' essays are not returned after being scored.

Chapter 4: The Written Essay, Personal Narrative & QEP

You must go through the entire testing process in order to qualify to be enlisted in the Foreign Service. This includes the multiple choice part of the test and the essay which tests your understanding of issues of national importance and your capacity to argue your position.

The FSOT'S Written Essay

The essay assesses your ability to analyze a given topic, organize your thoughts and develop and write a clear, coherent argument. The essay part of the test is 50 minutes long. You can pick a topic from a list of three. Common topics cover areas such as customs and culture, education and religion, economics and matters of finance, history and international affairs, issues of employment and social matters.

At the start of the test you will be issued with a booklet in which to write your essay by hand. Make sure you know enough about the topic, or have strong enough opinions to be able to create a clear, concise essay. You will be graded on how you analyze a particular topic, support your position and structure your sentences. Your grammar and syntax will also be assessed. Spelling and punctuation matter, but they are given less weight.

Sample FSOT Essay Topics

Now that you know what types of topics you're likely to see in the FSOT essay, you can begin to practice writing about them. For each of the topics listed below, create an outline comprising your main ideas on the subject matter. It's a good idea to write an essay just for practice. If any of the suggested topics are entirely new to you, consider researching them because they are each important in the field of Foreign Service and you need to have a reasonably broad understanding of them. One essay should take you 50 minutes or less to write.

Essay No. 1: Entertainers and Politics

Singers, actors and other entertainers frequently help raise money for their candidates of choice. However, some people believe entertainers have no place in politics. Others believe entertainers should be allowed to exercise their freedom of speech, including saying what they think of a particular candidate. In fact, some people see speaking out as a civic obligation. What is your personal view regarding the role of entertainers in politics? Do you think they exercise undue influence because of their fame and popularity? Do you think they have an undue advantage because of their convenient access to TV and other media? State your position and explain why that is what you believe.

Essay No. 2: The Concept of an Essay-Grading Computer

Owing to the increasing number of essays that require grading, some universities are experimenting with the use of computers to grade essays. Students don't necessarily like this idea. Some feel a machine can't possibly grasp the nuances of the argument they are making. Conversely, proponents of the machine-grading system feel that it's reasonable to use a computer because parameters can be set to determine if the student has addressed a particular question. These people also believe a computer can reasonably judge the structure of an essay. What is your view regarding the whole situation? State your position and explain why that is what you believe. If you disagree, offer solutions to the problem of too many essays for professors to thoroughly grade.

Essay No.3: The Delicate Issue of Cloning

Many arguments have been advanced regarding cloning, both for and against the procedure. Some people find the entire idea strange but don't know what to think about it. One viewpoint holds that there are long-term advantages of cloning when it comes to medical research so long as cloning is restricted solely to the scientific realm. The majority of people who are against cloning say it's subject to abuse, especially in the modern era where corporations are prone to corruption and dishonesty. Others also feel cloning may be abused amidst misunderstanding of the concept, process and implementation. Setting religious and moral considerations aside, what is your view on cloning? Who do you think should be given the mandate to determine if it is appropriate to legalize cloning—doctors, leaders of religious organizations or politicians? State your position and explain why that is what you believe.

Essay No.4: The Controversial Issue of Foreign Aid

Some politicians choose to avoid discussing foreign aid publicly because there are two sides to the argument and they don't want to antagonize either of them. Those in support of foreign aid believe that, being the world's wealthiest country, the U.S. has an obligation to help poor nations.

The people against foreign aid believe that the people who receive such assistance don't necessarily benefit from it. Moreover, there are many people who wonder what the U.S. gets in return for giving. What is your view regarding foreign aid? Do you support it? If so, to whom do you think it should be given? State your position and explain why that is what you believe.

The Personal Narrative & QEP

Once you have completed the FSOT form for your Personal Narrative (PN), it's sent to you and you are required to complete it in two weeks' time. Your completed PN form is then forwarded to a Qualifications Evaluation Panel (QEP), and their role is to read your

PN and provide feedback that determines if you're qualified to attend the Foreign Service Oral Assessment.

You should highlight your accomplishments in the PN, along with what lessons you've learned from your different experiences. Giving examples of various experiences you have gone through, demonstrating the use of skills a great FSO needs to have, is helpful.

You can expect your PN to be read in detail by every member of the QEP, which is comprised of Foreign Service Officers. Your chosen career track will be reviewed by a panel comprising officers experienced in that particular line of work.

Your file will be assessed on the basis of six precepts seen to predict your potential to be a successful Foreign Service Officer:

Leadership

The assessing panel needs to see your capacity to lead. Show them you're innovative, capable of excellent decision-making, work well as part of a team and are comfortable with and can handle dissent. Showing your inclination to offer community service also contributes to your image as a good leader who can help build and strengthen institutions.

Interpersonal skills

Good interpersonal skills can be demonstrated through your professional standards, your capacity to persuade, negotiate, adapt and represent other people's interests.

Communication skills

Writing is a key communication skill. You also need to be able to communicate clearly via speech *and* listening. An ability to network and/or speak foreign languages will all be assets.

Management skills

The assessing panel would like to see how effectively you operate in both normal and difficult situations. Assessors want to know how good you are at evaluating and managing situations. Providing proof that you can be a resourceful manager and supply excellent customer service will impress the panel.

Intellectual skills

The QEP screens your PN with a view to seeing how good you are at gathering information and analyzing it, thinking critically and being an active learner. The panel also looks for whether you're a viable trainee for leadership and management positions.

Substantive knowledge

You need to show you have a reasonable grasp of U.S. history, know how the government works and have a grasp of different cultures. You also need to be able to show concrete evidence for why you're qualified to pursue your chosen career track.

In short, when you complete your PN, your focus should be on the experiences you have personally had, and the above six precepts should serve as a helpful guide. Not only should the examples you cite be positive, but they should also emphasize your abilities. Remember to point out any relevant learning experiences you have had. In addition, show how these experiences can serve to make your career in the Foreign Service successful, particularly in the career track you have chosen. It is very important that you demonstrate you have relevant skills in your chosen career track, and that you have real interest in pursuing that path.

What the QEP Considers

A test administrator will forward your FSOT scores to the QEP, along with your registration package. The test administrator will not include personal details such as your age and ethnicity.

The panel applies the Total Candidate approach in making its assessment, which includes a look at your educational and work background, the responses you have provided to the questions asked in the PN, the skill level you have shown on the self-evaluation and your FSOT score.

One thing worth noting is that the score typically considered a pass is not preset when it comes to the QEP's evaluation. The panel looks at your entire file and those of other applicants and then determines the best candidates to invite for the oral assessment. The number of candidates the panel invites to go forward with the assessment also depends on the need for personnel in the respective career tracks.

Why there is No Preset Score

After the QEP completes its task, Pearson VUE will email you to inform you when you can access your results online. You'll need your login ID as well as the unique password used during registration. Going by applications submitted in recent years, the number of candidates applying to join the Foreign Office Service average over 20,000 annually. A much tinier fraction proceeds to the next stage where files are reviewed by the QEP, and ultimately just a couple hundred are successful in reaching the last stage where an oral assessment is done.

If you think you're a good candidate and have a serious interest in the Foreign Service but are not invited for the oral assessment, take heart and try again in the future. Sometimes you may score highly at a time when the government does not need many additional Foreign Service Officers, and so only a few candidates will be deemed successful.

What to Expect of the Foreign Service Oral Assessment

You are instructed via the official website to anticipate questions pertaining to leadership and communication, interpersonal and management skills, intellectual skills and a substantive amount of general knowledge. That scope is quite wide and thinking about it could be overwhelming, so focus instead on what you can easily prepare for.

For example, you can review your work history and pick out things you have accomplished that you can use during the assessment to highlight your abilities. You can also try to remember the experiences you have had that will specifically make you a better Foreign Service Officer. Consider how you can link your learning experiences to the particular career track you have chosen.

However you answer the questions posed to you during the Foreign Service Oral Assessment, don't lose sight of the fact that it's all about what a great diplomat you might someday make. Don't succumb to the temptation to mention all the awards or high-level positions you've ever received or held. Only mention any that could pertain to skills necessary in the Foreign Service. For example, just saying you were your college's rugby team captain doesn't show the panel of assessors you have the potential to become a good diplomat. Instead, you should specifically detail how a sports team captain needs elements of self-discipline and interpersonal strengths which will serve you well in the Foreign Service.

What to Include in Your Personal Narrative

It's important that the answers you provide are relevant to the questions asked. If you don't have many academic certifications to talk about, emphasize your other positive attributes, since success as a Foreign Service Officer requires more than just academic success.

Personal highlights you should consider mentioning include:

- a college degree or master's degree in a political field
- international travel
- positions of leadership you have held in the past that are associated with diplomacy
- proficiency in one or more foreign languages
- any hardships you have undergone that show you have the capacity to overcome adversity.

Remember to double-check your grammar and syntax before submitting your PN. If possible, give it to someone else to read and provide proofreading and feedback. At the end of the day, your PN should portray you as intelligent and a person with great potential to become a diplomat.

Validity of the FSOT Score

The passing score you receive is valid only for the period that was open for testing. This means if you pass the FSOT and receive the form for your PN but then fail to complete and send it back, your FSOT score will be invalid and you will not be able to appear before the QEP. This means, for example, that your FSOT results for February won't secure you an appointment for an oral assessment during the May testing window. You'll have to wait the 12-month window and retest. As a serious candidate, therefore, you should only take the FSOT if you're available to attend the oral assessment during the set dates for that testing window.

Modalities of Taking the Oral Assessment

If you're invited for the oral assessment, you will very likely take it from Washington, DC. These assessments go on throughout the year, and when there are resources available they're also held in other cities in the U.S.

For instance in February 2019, there were oral assessments carried out in San Francisco. Oral assessments were administered in Chicago in May 2019.

The oral assessment takes an entire day. There is a group exercise included in the assessment, a structured interview and a writing exercise in case management.

You should keep checking online for any changes to the oral assessment window and also the location, because these can be changed from time to time. Also if you can, it would be helpful to talk with a resident diplomat in an office near you, so that you can get better insight regarding oral assessments.

Qualities Expected of a Foreign Service Officer

Panelists reading candidates' PNs and listening to answers during the oral assessment specifically look for a set of particular qualities. The major attributes the QEP hopes to find in an aspiring FSO are explained here.

(1) Composure

Someone aspiring to become an FSO needs to be able to remain composed even in difficult situations. That is why during the interview process, both written and oral, you should demonstrate your capacity to remain calm, self-controlled and able to think on your feet as needed in swiftly changing situations.

(2) Cultural Adaptability

Cultural adaptability is your capacity not only to perform your work but also to communicate what you are doing effectively and harmoniously. You should be able to do all that in an environment where people from different cultures are involved, who may have value systems and political beliefs that differ from yours. Your capacity to work in harmony with others and to be effective in communicating with them and remain respectful and proactive in addressing differences is key to your success as an FSO and is definitely something the QED panel will be watching for.

(3) Experience and Motivation

Experience and motivation deal with the amount of knowledge and level of skill that you demonstrate, as well as other qualities you have gleaned from prior work experience. The assessors will be looking to see whether your skill set matches the job and whether you're motivated to be an excellent FSO.

(4) Information Integration and Analysis

As an FSO you'll need to be able to absorb and retain information of a complex nature derived from varied sources. You are also expected to be able to make reasoned decisions after you have analyzed and synthesized the available information. You should be able to recall details of meetings and events without having to refer to notes.

(5) Initiative and Leadership

The government defines initiative and leadership as the capacity to recognize and assume full responsibility for any work expected to be done by a group of which you are a member. You must take responsibility and persist in completing the task before you, regardless of challenges. You're also expected to influence group activity in a manner that shapes both its actions and opinions. This shows the panel that you'll be able to motivate people working with you.

(6) Judgment

Judgment in the context of an FSO means your capacity to be appropriate and practical when weighing different merits relative to one another, and to be able to gauge them against competing demands.

(7) Objectivity and Integrity

You need to show the assessors you can be fair, honest and avoid deceit, favoritism and discrimination. You must show the panel that you're able to operate without personal bias or prejudices influencing the actions you take or how you work.

(8) Oral Communication

The best way to show the panel that you're great at communicating orally is to speak in a concise, fluent manner. Your grammar should obviously be good, and your speech should be organized and precise. It's important that you demonstrate how you can adapt your communication style as necessary to different situations.

(9) Planning and Organizing

Show the assessors you know how to effectively prioritize and organize tasks, approaching work in a systematic fashion. You also need to make clear that you are capable of managing well with insufficient resources, which might sometimes be the case in an overseas embassy or consulate.

(10)   Resourcefulness

As far as the State Department is concerned, resourcefulness is gauged with regard to your capacity to creatively formulate alternatives or solutions to problems. You need to show the panel that you can be flexible when there's a need for you to respond to unforeseen circumstances.

(11)   Capacity to Work with Other People

If you aspire to be an FSO, the interviewing panel must see you're capable of working well with other people. They need to view you as someone who can contribute constructively while cooperating with others and working with them in harmony. In short, you need to come across as a capable team player. You should be able to show that you can engage in positive relationships and win other people's confidence. Being able to appreciate humor and use it appropriately is also a plus.

(12)　Written Communication

The U.S. State Department expects all FSOs to be good at communicating in writing. You should be able to write in an organized manner, concisely, correctly (grammar, syntax, etc.), effectively and persuasively within a limited time frame.

(13)　Qualitative Analysis

In qualitative analysis, the interviewing panel assesses how well you identify, compile and analyze important data and then make correct deductions. You should demonstrate your ability to detect trends or patterns formed by important data, and to carry out simple mathematical calculations.

Chapter 5: How the State Department Clears Candidates

Candidates who pass the FSOT oral assessment are issued with an employment offer contingent on a medical clearance. Until this is completed, there is no guarantee of a job. Candidates who have gotten this far have to wait for the Medical Services office in the U.S. State Department to determine that they are medically fit and capable of serving overseas.

The Process of Medical Clearance

Many posts available in the Foreign Service are situated in areas of the world that are remote, and medical services there are sometimes very limited. Every candidate must therefore satisfy rigorous medical standards to reduce the possibilities of health crises in areas where medical attention may not be immediately available.

A candidate's medical history will be reviewed thoroughly, and a physical exam will be performed. Candidates will be asked about their own assessment of their medical fitness and ability to serve in remote places overseas.

Once candidates have received the conditional employment offer, they are also given the required exam form and instructed on the health-care practitioner to take it to. This could be an MD, Doctor of Osteopathic Medicine, nurse practitioner or physician's assistant.

Scheduling of Medical Exam Date

If you have passed all the stages of the FSO interview including the oral assessment and require a medical assessment, you must schedule a suitable date for that depending on how far you live from Washington, DC. If you reside within 50 miles of the city, your appointment should be at the Medical Services office within the State Department. Otherwise you can be examined by your own physician or have the examination done at your city's State Department.

State Department's Authority with Regards to Eligibility

After candidates' medical insurance has paid for the appropriate part of medical services, the Medical Services office authorizes the State Department to release payments for medical exams conducted outside the department. Candidates due for medical examinations are given a 90-day window within which to complete the process. The U.S. Medical Services Department has the final word when it comes to determining if a given candidate is medically suitable to take up a government post in any part of the world.

Candidates who receive a Class One medical clearance are deemed fit to serve in areas of extreme isolation, including those where air transportation and other transportation services are limited. These are candidates who have shown they can survive and operate optimally where internet and telecommunication services are unreliable, and where the postal service and other forms of delivery are inefficient.

There are instances where the state department can greenlight a candidate to serve in the U.S. or a specified location outside the country, yet deem the same individual ineligible to serve in other places. This means the state department doesn't give the candidate a Class One medical clearance.

Why a Pre-Employment Medical Evaluation is Necessary

There are countries known to have poor infrastructure, including minimal health-care systems and poor sanitation, an unreliable electricity supply and/or a poor supply of water. Some countries are also prone to infectious and communicable illnesses such as malaria and dengue fever, gastrointestinal illnesses, typhoid, rabies and encephalitis. Any of these and others can be fatal where there are no medical facilities available.

In some parts of the world, hospitals are few and far apart, and if there is an emergency room in the vicinity it might be poorly equipped, sometimes missing ventilators and defibrillators. Other essentials missing for medical emergencies could include blood banks and vital medications. Some areas are also politically unstable and could add to the problems with accessing needed medical care.

If people who are not strong enough both medically and psychologically are deployed to those tough areas, their stress levels could rise significantly and make it hard for them to be successful at their jobs. That is why the State Department chooses only to deploy FSOs with Class One medical clearances to such areas.

Only the FSO is medically evaluated. If you join the Foreign Service and have family members that will travel with you, their medical status will be not be evaluated as a pre-condition for your employment.

Nevertheless, whenever such family members are being sponsored by the government to travel out of the country in the company of their related government employees, they have to get medical clearance first. While medical status of a family member does not restrict the FSO's deployment, if you have a Class One clearance and a family member isn't cleared, they won't be able to travel with you. That's something really important to consider when pursuing a career in the Foreign Service.

Granting of Special Clearance

There are rare instances when the Foreign Service Director General, otherwise referred to as the designee, can decide to grant a worldwide availability waiver to a candidate who fails to qualify for a Class One clearance.

Process For Getting Security Clearance

Although it's mandatory for a candidate to get a medical clearance from the State Department, that still doesn't entitle him or her to an actual employment letter. As an aspiring FSO you'll need to also pass a security clearance in order to be fully confirmed into the service.

Before such clearance is granted to a candidate, the State Department works with other government agencies, federal and local, gathering and assessing relevant information associated with the candidate.

At the end of the investigation the State Department will determine the suitability of the candidate to be appointed to the Foreign Service. The same results help to determine if the person will receive a top-secret security clearance.

Factors Considered for Security Clearance

The major factors taken into account during a security clearance are:

- failure to clear loans government loans
- failure to pay taxes
- refusal to register for Selective Service
- poor credit history or a history of bankruptcy
- an unfavorable employment record
- criminal record or a history of violating the law
- history of alcohol or drug abuse
- dishonorable military discharge.

Sometimes a candidate could be fine for an FSO post as far as the factors mentioned above are concerned, yet have his or her clearance delayed because of matters of association. For example, if you have dual citizenship your clearance might take longer than other candidates. Other factors that might delay your clearance because they necessitate more investigation include:

- having traveled extensively
- being educated overseas

- having resided overseas
- having been employed overseas
- having foreign contacts
- having a spouse who was born overseas
- having close family members who are not U.S. citizens.

A background check of your history and status includes interviewing your contacts, both current and past. Your former supervisors and also co-workers may also be interviewed. This information is helpful to those thinking of taking up a career in the Foreign Service because if you have a personal history that is likely to deter your clearance, you may want to choose a different career that's not so selective instead of spending time applying for a job you're unlikely to get.

Role of the Suitability Review Panel

After you've passed all components of the FSOT and have medical and security clearance, you're still not a confirmed FSO. Your file needs to be read by a Suitability Review Panel.

This panel reads through your documentation—not your medical records; those are private—to finalize the decision as to whether you should be employed by the Foreign Service and will be able to carry out your responsibilities in a manner that will help promote U.S. interests abroad.

The review panel evaluates a candidate's conduct and social standing in totality, and it is on the basis of these findings that they determine if an individual is fit to be a representative of the U.S. abroad. If the Suitability Review Panel doesn't find you an acceptable candidate, your road to becoming an FSO ends right there.

Specific Factors Considered by the Suitability Review Panel

The following information will help you assess yourself before embarking on the FSO testing journey. The Suitability Review Panel will be looking at all these things, so carefully consider these potential red flags:

- a record of misconduct in places you have worked before, including poor performance or difficulty interacting with fellow workers.
- a criminal record or association with criminals
- dishonesty and/or misrepresentation of yourself on your FSOT documentation
- a record of drug or alcohol abuse.

Furthermore, if the Suitability Review Panel has any reason to doubt your loyalty to the American government you will not be given an FSO appointment.

Another factor the panel considers is whether you come across as having poor judgment or lack discretion. In order to carry out your responsibilities as an FSO you need to have good judgment of people, situations and other such factors. You also need to be trustworthy, in particular when it comes to making appropriate financial decisions.

Chapter 6: Matters Pertaining to the Hiring Register

If you successfully complete all the requirements discussed in the previous chapters then your name will be placed on a hiring register according to your rank as per your chosen career track and your score on the oral assessment.

An important point to note is that being placed on the hiring register is no guarantee for a job as an FSO. Actual hiring is dependent on the government's need for staff in the Foreign Service. Another significant point is that the position you rank at when first put in the register is dynamic. It is bound to keep changing as other successful candidates are added to the register. Depending on their scores, you will either rank higher than before or lower, as those above you get deployed to their stations. In short, employment as FSO is not done on a first come, first served basis but on the basis of how good your scores are. For that reason, some candidates who have been put on the hiring register take longer to be employed than others.

Nevertheless, your name can only remain on the hiring register for 18 months. If you're not appointed to a job in that time frame, your name will be removed from the register.

How to Raise Your Ranking in the Hiring Register

There are candidates who complete all the many FSO requirements and yet end up ranking differently in the register even when their scores are similar.

U.S. veterans are given special consideration in the recruitment process, automatically earning Veteran Preference points. Other candidates rank higher than others on the basis of their capacity to converse in diverse foreign languages.

Normally after successfully completing your oral assessment, you are advised on the factors that are likely to rank you higher on the hiring register. If you know your ranking won't be high, you may opt to retake the FSOT after 12 months with the hope of performing better with the advantage of your experience having already undergone the process once. It's important to note that once you decide to retake the FSOT, you'll have to repeat every single step of the process including the medical and security clearance and Suitability Review Panel. Retaking the FSOT also gives you a chance to change your career track to one you think might allow you to rank higher on the hiring register.

Events after Being Recommended for Hiring

Once you're identified as a suitable candidate for an open position, you will be sent an employment offer. Usually you will be required to go to Washington, DC, on short notice, often just a couple of weeks, to begin training.

When to Defer Acceptance of Employment Offer

While candidates are expected to be excited about receiving offers of employment, sometimes the circumstances at the time you receive your employment offer might be unsuitable, whether for personal reasons or others.

Fortunately, you have room to decline your first offer, in which case your name will be retained on the hiring register awaiting another employment chance in the future. However, if you are sent a second offer for employment and you turn it down, you can no longer remain on the hiring register, and your name will immediately be removed.

There are a few other instances when you may be allowed to defer your acceptance for a job offer, mainly if you're serving in the military and can't just leave duty at a moment's notice, or if you're on government duty overseas.

Formal Training of FSOs

When you receive an employment offer to work in the Foreign Service and report to Washington, DC, your career begins with a six-week orientation program known as the A-100 course. The course is based in Arlington, Virginia, where the National Foreign Affairs Training Center is.

At the beginning of the orientation, trainers focus on introducing recruits to the State Department's structure and function. They explain the role the department plays in development and implementation of U.S. foreign policy. The new employees are also helped to understand their employment terms. They're given training that enhances the core skills required by employees in the Foreign Service.

New employees will visit Capitol Hill and other different federal agencies. They'll also train for two days at a conference center near the Arlington facility.

During their training in Arlington, VA, new employees listen to presentations by guest speakers as well as officials from the U.S. State Department. The A-100 course incorporates a number of exercises of a practical nature, along with case studies. After successfully completing the orientation course, newly recruited FSOs receive their initial assignments, which determine the kind of specialized training that they will require going forward. After that initial assignment, some FSOs might be trained in consular affairs, others in affairs of a political-economic nature, resource management or public diplomacy.

There are times an FSO might be required to undergo language training for six to nine months. Generally, newly recruited FSOs can expect their training to last as little as three months, but it can be as long as an entire year before they are deployed to their respective stations overseas.

Candidates Who Get Time Concessions

Some factors are accorded extra weight by the U.S. government when deciding if individual candidates should be granted extra time in the assessment process. People on active service in the military and veterans are allowed to request to be exempted from the timeline restriction. They can therefore be given extra time within which to schedule their oral assessment.

Candidates in this category are expected to notify the Board of Examiners (BEX) of when they're discharged from military service and then proceed to reschedule their oral assessment. This needs to happen within six months of leaving the military.

As noted earlier, other candidates who have an added advantage with regards to the hiring process are veterans, as they qualify for additional points that rank them higher on the hiring register than ordinary candidates with the same test scores. However, they need to provide Form DD 214 as evidence that they are really U.S. veterans. In the absence of this form, there are other forms of certifications that can attest to a veteran's eligibility. In technical terms, a five-point standing earns a veteran 0.175 while a 10-point standing earns veteran 0.35.

In every case, the awarding of points is done after the candidate has passed the oral assessment. That's when candidates are advised on how to claim their extra points. Veterans who are eligible for hire as FSOs and have their names ranked on the hiring register can be appointed as long as they're not 65. If a veteran is appointed who is between the ages of 60 and 65, he or she qualifies to serve for a five-year period before mandatory retirement is required.

Advantage of Knowing a Foreign Language

It's not mandatory that an FSO know a foreign language. Being good at English is good enough when working for the U.S. government. However, knowledge of an additional foreign language makes you more competitive among other candidates and enhances your chances of being hired. Your proficiency in a foreign language earns you a few additional points, and can raise your chances of being put on the registry of potential FSO employees.

It's important to note that just because you can speak a foreign language that doesn't automatically give you more points. There's an additional test component required. You earn a language score by taking the relevant Foreign Service Officer Language test by phone, and once this score is recorded you're granted the appropriate points as per the set scale. Obviously, the higher your score in the language test, the better.

Any candidate with knowledge of a foreign language qualifies for .17 extra points. Among the languages that can earn you these points are:

- Chinese or Mandarin
- Arabic
- Hindi
- Persian or Dari
- Persian or Farsi
- Korean
- Pashto
- Urdu.

Candidates earn extra points if they attain a speaking level 3 on the phone test.

If you take the telephone test and attain a level 2 for your ability to speak, then you qualify to get .17 extra points. Normally once you pass your oral assessment, you should expect to be sent a link that leads you to the Career Candidate Handbook, and here you will find guidelines on how to make arrangements for your telephone-based test.

This test is carried out by the Foreign Service Institute (FSI) which falls under the State Department. You can take the language test immediately, without having to wait till you are included on the hiring register.

If you want to earn even more points, you can take a two-hour person-to-person speaking test that also involves reading. The Foreign Service Institute is in charge of conducting this second test and you will have to pay for it yourself including accommodation in Washington, DC, travel expenses, and any other costs associated with the testing. If you succeed in attaining a score of 3 in speaking and 2 in reading, which is abbreviated as S3/R2, you qualify for .38 aggregate bump-up language points.

If you succeed in getting a rating of 2 in speaking and 1 in reading, abbreviated as S2/R1, you qualify for .25 aggregate bump-up points. The candidates who choose to do an in-person test and fail to attain a S2/R1 as the minimum (known as generalist candidates) will not receive any bonus points. This is inclusive of any points they might have already earned by taking the telephone test.

Points are given only for a single language, but candidates can choose to test for an additional language if they don't pass the first language test. They can also choose to test in an additional language in case it has a greater point value. After six months, a candidate can retake the language test. If you fail the language test twice, you have to wait a full year before retesting again.

The validity of the telephone-based language score lasts eighteen months, while that of any in-person language score lasts five years.

As for security clearance, you're likely to require one specific to the particular country in which that language is used. If you're a generalist candidate and are seeking .38 bump-up language points, there is a condition that you accept to hold a position of service where the language is needed one time in the course of your first two deployments, and one time after you have attained middle-level grades within the Foreign Service.

In such cases you must fulfill your promised second deployment before you can be considered to serve in a senior capacity in the Foreign Service. If you're a generalist candidate and qualify for .25 bump-up points, you're required to agree to offer service one time in the course of your first two deployments in a post that calls for the use of your chosen foreign language.

There is more helpful information pertaining to language at http://www.govtilr.org. Log in and click "speaking." The site even has a language tool you can use for self-assessment.

Assistance Offered to FSO Candidates Who Have a Disability

If you have passed the FSOT and have a disability, and you need accommodations made once you have been appointed, the Office of Accessibility & Accommodations Disability & Reasonable Accommodations Division will help ensure you receive reasonable accommodations.

In order to fit in this category of FSO employees, you have to first satisfy every requirement for anyone working in the Foreign Service. The division caters to all state employees with disabilities and is guided by federal law. It also facilitates candidates with disabilities' access to the FSOT, including providing them with appropriate accommodations when they are required to take the oral assessment.

Test 1: Questions

(1) As a member of a management team that seeks to enhance its effectiveness and forge a great relationship with its employees while also trying to optimize the performance of the organization, you could make use of:

(A) Executive education

(B) Upward feedback

(C) Job rotation

(D) Mentoring

(2) If the US Bureau of Labor Statistics decides to hire someone who has no disability even when a more qualified individual who uses a wheelchair also applied for the job, the bureau will have violated the:

(A) Rehabilitation Act of 1973

(B) Civil Rights Act of 1964

(C) Military Veterans Act of 2011

(D) None of the above

(3) An employer can legally ask a pregnant woman to:

(A) Shift from the front desk to avoid direct contact with clients

(B) Produce medical evidence showing that the pregnancy is making her incapable of working, thus causing her to require leave

(C) Take a minimum of six weeks leave of absence after she gives birth

(D) None of the above

(4) Per Title VII of the Civil Rights Act of 1964, a US employer can be sued if:

(A) An employee faces unwelcome advances even if there is no economic fallout

(B) An employee makes a coworker uncomfortable by telling jokes with sexual connotations

(C) A manager makes demonstrative contact of a physical nature with a subordinate who is of the same gender

(D) All of the above situations can lead to a legal suit

(5) Any time a manager gets personally involved in order to motivate employees, there is a risk to employees:

(A) Whose self-esteem is low and who are unable to meet high performance expectations

(B) Whose only commitment to set goals is verbal

(C) Who like making commitments within a group set-up but not on an individual level

(D) Who are overconfident about their capacity to perform

(6) Performance management can be replaced by another method referred to as:

(A) The quota system

(B) A traditional appraisal system

(C) Merit pay

(D) A quarterly or annual bonus schedule

(7) According to the FSLA, any employee who is exempt and earns $28.50 an hour while working 45 hours a week should receive a paycheck amounting to:

(A) $1,282.50

(B) $1,710.00

(C) $1,923.75

(D) $1,353.75

(8) The reason employers are expected to fill in form I-9 for every employee is to verify:

(A) That the person is eligible to work in the United States

(B) That the person meets the minimum age set for employees

(C) That the person does not have any criminal record

(D) That all employees pay their direct income tax

(9) It is incumbent upon the manager to see to it that every employee is given a job description that is clear and accurate. If this does not happen, the employer could be liable for:

(A) Escalating costs on the payroll

(B) Legal suits associated with violating the ADA

(C) Suits under all laws protecting the employee

(D) Legal suit for sexual harassment against employees

(10) There is sometimes some vagueness when it comes to employee appraisals. A good way to remedy this is by supplementing the standard company forms with:

(A) Better forms that different companies use

(B) Other forms with the rating scales designed by the respective managers

(C) Written comments with more clearly explained rating scales

(D) Additional verbal appraisal of an employee

(11) Skewing appraisals positively just because employees are performing well in some areas should be avoided. This tendency is referred to as:

(A) Recency effect

(B) Central tendency effect

(C) Halo effect

(D) Leniency bias

(12) During the process of evaluation or appraisal, which of the areas listed below would be considered soft in regard to employees being likely to feel personally offended?

(A) Production quotas

(B) Sales figures

(C) Teamwork

(D) Absenteeism

(13) If a manager focuses on _____, he or she is very likely to successfully motivate employees in the long-term.

(A) Reminding employees of the importance of great job performance

(B) Enhancing competition among employees

(C) Understanding both the goals and interests of employees

(D) Issuing bonuses plus other incentives on the basis of performance

(14) Managers making use of the Pygmalion Effect often succeed in getting employees to perform well by:

(A) Showing them they are very capable of achieving set goals

(B) Developing teams capable of handling several big projects as opposed to having individuals working within a hierarchy

(C) Setting ambiguous expectations to encourage employees to be original and creative

(D) Always attaching some incentive of a financial nature to job performance

(15) On the basis of Maslow's Hierarchy of Needs, people attach more importance or put more emphasis upon:

(A) Needs of a cognitive nature

(B) Self-actualization

(C) Needs of a physiological nature

(D) A sense of belonging

(16) Supervising employee productivity and how employees perform activities on a daily basis is the generally accepted role of management, but there needs to be a balance because micromanaging employees can often end up:

(A) Enhancing performance

(B) Stifling inventiveness

(C) Breaking the flow of communication

(D) Raising morale

(17) A person who actively listens manifests all traits listed below except:

(A) Often completing other people's sentences

(B) Being aware of and controlling biases

(C) Providing feedback while refraining from interrupting others

(D) Planning a response to give after the other person has completed speaking

(18) Regarding employees' personal lives, managers should:

(A) Take an interest and then show their concern where necessary while empathizing with the employees

(B) Urge subordinates to address their colleagues' personal problems

(C) Remain unconcerned but make recommendations for the employee to be assisted as needed by human resources

(D) Regularly make inquiries in order to establish the existing problems

(19) Going by the Civil Rights Act's Title VII, it is illegal for an employer to inhibit the religious practice of any employee when at the workplace unless:

(A) The employer fails to observe the employee's religious holidays

(B) The employee's religious practices make the work environment unsafe

(C) The employee's religious beliefs call for the employer to accommodate grooming

(D) The employee and the employer have disagreements over the employee's beliefs related to his or her religion.

(20)   Suppose you have recently established a management job that has more than 500 employees, and you find out that there are some practices in your company that are not compliant with the Equal Pay Act of 1963 and all other amendments associated with it. You could take all the steps listed below in order to remedy the situation except:

(A) Ensure you do not succumb to the demands of the labor union or any contracts bound to violate the statute

(B) Ensure you raise pay so that such increases lead to both male and female employees earning equal pay for the same job

(C) Reduce the pay for employees earning unduly higher wages than others of a different gender doing similar jobs while trying to equalize employees' remuneration

(D) Set pay increases in the future on the basis of a well-designed system that entails merit and seniority as well as performance-based quotas

(21) When as a manager you want to reduce stress associated with work in your workforce, you can use a cost-effective and easy-to-follow strategy, which entails:

(A) Lessening employee responsibilities

(B) Practicing a strategy of planning ahead that reduces the need to manage a crisis

(C) Creating a work area that has an open layout so employees are able to see and hear one another as they work

(D) Emphasizing a competitive attitude among employees through an increment in the incentives given for performance while trying to enhance productivity

(22)   When it comes to designing jobs, both managers and employees can reduce stress by doing all of the following things except:

(A) Creating channels of communication to address immediate needs and those likely to occur in the future

(B) Applying ergonomic designs as needed to employee equipment

(C) Establishing working hours and shift changes that lead to the highest level of profits for the company

(D) Creating a list of specific requirements that allows for the recruitment of employees who are most appropriate for vacant posts

(23)   When as an employer you involve different people in an employee evaluation, such as fellow coworkers, supervisors or customers, such a process is referred to as:

(A) 360° feedback

(B) All-in-one evaluation

(C) Knowledge management

(D) Job coaching

(24)   When it is time to interview a person for a job, aptitude tests are often carried out in the early stages of the process to evaluate:

(A) The candidate's level of specialized and technical skills

(B) The candidate's traits or general character

(C) The candidate's IQ or level of intelligence

(D) The candidate's general capacity to reason and write well

(25)   You are invited to be part of an ad hoc committee formed to see what changes are appropriate for the company's benefits package. Such a committee very likely will:

(A) Meet on a regular basis until the completion of the necessary changes

(B) Meet just once and address the entire issue in one go

(C) Be made permanent to keep addressing all the issues that affect employee benefits

(D) Keep liaising with the board as it holds regular meetings

(26)   When two employees clash during meetings and make their colleagues uncomfortable, what is the best action to take?

(A) Fire or transfer one of the employees involved in the clashes, specifically the one you consider of lesser value to the business

(B) Counsel the clashing employees on better ways of working together and keep monitoring their progress going forward

(C) Tell the employees to sort out the situation and leave them to it without getting involved

(D) Immediately reassign the two employees to different areas of work

(27)   Researchers in the field of psychology, including Abraham Maslow and Kurt Goldstein, have explored the theory of self-actualization. Choose the option below that best supports this theory.

(A) An employee receives a bonus after meeting a sales quota

(B) An employee works consistently for one company for 30 years, during which he rises in rank from an office clerk to the position of regional vice president

(C) An employee consciously chooses to sabotage a project being undertaken by a team that he belongs to as a way of avenging himself against his senior

(D) An employee is poorly evaluated owing to his tendency to abuse alcohol

(28)   The discipline in which people learn about human behavior within the workplace, both as individuals and as groups, is commonly referred to as:

(A) Organizational or industrial psychology

(B) Developmental or educational psychology

(C) Social psychology

(D) Applied psychology

(29)   Under the Civil Rights Act's Title IV, any company whose practice of hiring employees includes _____ violates the law.

(A) Hiring only degree holders

(B) Hiring only candidates whose educational qualifications match the job at hand

(C) Coding résumés/applications according to candidates' race or gender

(D) Carrying out an aptitude test for every candidate

(30)   There are different ways of keeping employees motivated. Among them are two significant categories, namely factors of hygiene and motivators. Identify the choice that falls under the category of motivators: one that cannot succeed unless needs of a basic nature or factors of hygiene are fulfilled.

(A) Holiday time

(B) Advancement

(C) Salary

(D) Job security

(31) Some managers believe it is possible to divide management styles into two groups, namely Theory X and Theory Y. The latter is said to be motivating and emphasizes ordinary collaboration between managers and their staff, while welcoming input and feedback from employees for the sake of making decisions. A manager of this type is very likely:

(A) To constantly evaluate employees by way of a system of downward appraisal

(B) To keep rotating chairmanship of the company's regular staff meetings

(C) To reprimand employees in public when they fail to encourage their colleagues

(D) To establish department goals in a unilateral manner

(32)   Assume there is a group of employees working for you as a team on a project estimated to take six months. When you decide you need to reinforce ownership of team member tasks, the best way to go about it is:

(A) To replace individual members of the team who do not meet the set goals

(B) To delegate fresh tasks to individual members of the team in order to differentiate their experience

(C) To countermand any questionable decisions the team has made

(D) To require daily progress reports and daily meetings with the team leader

(33)   There are some situations that qualify an employee for the Family and Medical Leave Act (FMLA). Which of the options below is such a situation?

(A) Tom, who has been working in the main office of a big government agency that employs several hundred people, has requested to be allowed to take one month's leave to undergo heart surgery.

(B) Mary has been working for a big corporation with more than 1,000 employees for over two years now, and she has asked her employer to grant her two months leave to attend to her ailing grandmother who lives in a different state.

(C) Jones has been working for six years at a vehicle repair shop that has 16 employees. He has requested that his employer grant him four weeks of leave as soon as his pregnant wife delivers.

(D) Aisha has been working for close to one year as manager of a national restaurant chain that has 10 branches within a 50-mile radius. She has recently adopted a child and has consequently requested three weeks of leave.

(34)   All of the options below except one are in compliance with the Americans with Disabilities Act (ADA). Which is the exception?

(A) Requiring every candidate who applies for a job to undergo a medical examination to assess his or her capacity to carry out those job aspects that are of a physical nature

(B) Refusing to hire a candidate because of a disability that could lower the department's production quota

(C) Asking a candidate to clarify his or her physical limitations due to a visible physical disability

(D) Making drug screening compulsory for all candidates before they can be considered for employment

(35) According to the 1978 Civil Service Reform Act, government agencies that are establishing merit pay systems should take into account all of the options listed below except:

(A) The local rates

(B) Excellent performance

(C) Rating scales used by employers within the private sector

(D) A person's marital status

(36) Any manager in a given government agency is failing to comply with the 1978 Civil Service Reform Act if he or she designs a system of appraisal for an employee that:

(A) Calls for employees to be evaluated on an annual basis

(B) Calls for immediate termination of employees rated poorly during evaluation

(C) Encourages employees to participate in setting standards as well as goals

(D) Does all of the above

(37) Which of the management styles listed below is very good for managing highly trained professionals who are very creative and highly self-motivated?

(A) Laissez-faire

(B) Passive autocratic

(C) Paternalistic

(D) Directive autocratic

(38)   When you want to assess a job applicant for _____, you might ask a question such as, "Can you remember a colleague in your last place of work who you found difficult to work with, and what can you tell me about how you coped with that challenge?"

(A) How well he or she handles stressful situations

(B) How much he or she is interested in being hired for the job

(C) Her or his level of motivation

(D) How suitable he or she is for the job in terms of the skills required

(39)   The management team has decided to implement a Continuous Improvement Plan (CIP), the kind that Edward Deming suggested is best to help a department fulfill long-term goals. On the basis of the CIP, you will likely:

(A) Prefer quantity more than quality

(B) Create a document that specifies the actions you want done

(C) Opt to ignore appraising the status of your plan on a regular basis

(D) Do none of the above

(40)   If you decide against hiring a candidate on the grounds that he or she is limited in English language proficiency, your omission could be a violation of the Civil Rights Act, Title VII unless:

(A) All other company employees are required to speak fluent English and there is a written policy to that effect

(B) Speaking fluent English plays a major role in maintaining the safety of the work environment

(C) The candidate is a foreigner

(D) None of the above

(41) The tendency of media to choose specific points in a story to promote their definition of the problem highlighted or even interpretation of a causal nature and moral assessment is referred to as:

(A) Setting of agenda

(B) Priming

(C) Framing

(D) Cultivation

(42)   There used to be a policy that required media presenters to provide diversified perspectives to controversial issues to avoid one point of view becoming dominant. However, this policy was repealed in 1987 by the US Congress. That original policy was the :

(A) Media bias rule

(B) Communications decency act

(C) Equal time rule

(D) Fairness doctrine

(43)   Some of the biggest _____ based in the United States include Weber Shandwick, Ketchum Inc., FleishmanHillard Inc. and Hill+Knowlton Strategies.

(A) Media conglomerates

(B) Media research firms

(C) Public relations agencies

(D) Newspaper chains

(44)   Among the entities listed below, one reports to the US Congress directly and does not consult with the US State Department in its operations. Which is it?

(A) Educational & Cultural Affairs Bureau

(B) International Department

(C) Public Affairs Bureau

(D) The Broadcasting Board of Governors

(45)   The Smith-Mundt Act, which is basically the United States' Information & Educational Exchange Act of 1948 (IEEA), deters the government from:

(A) Giving leeway to international broadcasters that receive sponsorship from foreign governments

(B) Purposely giving false or misleading information to a foreign audience

(C) Releasing information meant for foreign audiences to audiences in the United States

(D) Taking part in cultural or educational exchange programs that involve governments not signatory to the UN Declaration on Human Rights

(46)   The citizens of the United States are prohibited from listening to or reading certain materials meant for the outreach of public diplomacy owing to some acts passed by Congress. These acts include:

(A) Percy-Abzug

(B) Fulbright-Hayes

(C) McCain-Feingold

(D) Smith-Mundt

(47) One of the entities or programs listed below is an official American government body involved in public diplomacy initiatives. Which one is it?

(A) The Business for Diplomatic Action

(B) The Edward R. Murrow Center of Public Diplomacy

(C) The International Visitors Leadership Program

(D) The National Endowment for Democracy

(48) During the 1960s and 1970s, Tom Wolfe, Joan Didion, Gay Talese and others like them were known to often take their sources' point of view when they wrote. That kind of reporting was referred to as:

(A) Muckraking

(B) Civic journalism

(C) Investigative journalism

(D) New journalism

(49) How attractive a culture and its values are can increase a country's importance on the international scene. Which of the terms listed below is often used to describe such an impact?

(A) Psychological operations

(B) National branding

(C) The CNN impact

(D) Soft power

(50)   Suppose there are editorials in a newspaper called Lapatria condemning the United States' refusal to provide a country with assistance. Which option listed below is best taken by an officer serving in the foreign office?

(A) Talk to the US State Department about increasing assistance to the country

(B) Get booklets printed and issue press releases making it known that the United States is interested in enhancing philanthropic initiatives in both the country's private and public sectors

(C) Initiate lobbying with a view to having USAID increase its support to the country

(D) Hold a press conference and strongly denounce the criticism

(51) Which of the following US presidents served two non-consecutive terms?

(A) Grover Cleveland

(B) Franklin Roosevelt

(C) Theodore Roosevelt

(D) Zachary Taylor

(52)   The government's reason for creating The Warren Commission was:

(A) To investigate prominent government officials for perceived communist views

(B) To investigate allegations leveled against President Andrew Johnson that ended up with him being impeached

(C) To investigate the viability of buying Alaska

(D) To investigate the assassination of John F. Kennedy

(53)   The Scopes Trial revolved around:

(A) Press freedom

(B) Education offered by investors in the private sector

(C) Teaching of evolution in US schools

(D) Reciting the pledge of allegiance in US schools

(54)   Who was the Roman emperor involved in building a huge wall running across the northern part of Britain in AD 122?

(A) Emperor Hadrian

(B) Emperor Augustus

(C) Emperor Nero

(D) Emperor Marcus Aurelius

(55)   Who wrote what is referred to as "the 95 theses"?

(A) St. Augustus

(B) Martin Luther

(C) Henry D. Thoreau

(D) Voltaire

(56)   The US Constitution has _____ amendments so far.

(A) 25

(B) 10

(C) 16

(D) 27

(57) Choose the option that best describes who Stamford Raffles was.

(A) The founder of the Malay Peninsula

(B) The captain who led the ship that began the initial Opium War

(C) Singapore's founder

(D) The first explorer from the West to visit Southeast Asia

(58) _____ fought against the combined forces of Uruguay, Brazil and Argentina from 1864 to 1870?

(A) Chile

(B) Columbia

(C) Venezuela

(D) Paraguay

(59) Who founded Afghanistan?

(A) Ahmad Shah Abdali

(B) Zaman Shah Abdali

(C) Akbar Khan

(D) Timur Shah Abdali

(60) The belief that it is good to raise taxes in order to assist the poor exemplifies:

(A) A passive economic statement

(B) A positive economic statement

(C) A normative economic statement

(D) An objective economic statement

(61) From an economic perspective, the items listed below, apart from one, can be shown in a PPF. Which is that exception?

(A) Consumer preference

(B) The impact of enhanced modern technology

(C) The effect of increased cost of machinery for production of one of the goods

(D) Opportunity cost when one of the goods is produced in more quantity

(62) The way price mechanism works is mostly through:

(A) Government expenditures and welfare benefits

(B) Incentives and signaling

(C) Taxes as well as subsidies

(D) Maximum and minimum prices

(63) Where is the Cordillera de los Frailes, located within the cities of Potosi and Oruro, geographically situated?

(A) Bolivia

(B) France

(C) Spain

(D) Portugal

(64)   There are _____ countries bordering China.

(A) 17

(B) 12

(C) 19

(D) 14

(65)   The country with the biggest population on the African continent is:

(A) Nigeria

(B) Egypt

(C) Ethiopia

(D) South Africa

(66)   The mountain considered highest in South America when its height is taken right from sea level up to the top is:

(A) Huascarán

(B) Ojos del Salado

(C) Aconcagua

(D) Monte Pissis

(67)   There is a capital city in Latin America that was developed in the region where Tenochtitlan, the capital of the Aztec Empire, existed. Which is that city?

(A) San José

(B) Mexico City

(C) Panama City

(D) Georgetown

(68)   It is more appropriate to maintain focus on intangible rewards and corporate culture as opposed to adherence to stringent rules when:

(A) The work involved entails creativity and self-direction

(B) The tasks involved are of a repetitive nature and require low skills

(C) The results expected from the work being done are standard

(D) The work being done can be evaluated and measured with precision

(69)   It would be beneficial to use performance management as a substitute for:

(A) Bonus schedules–quarterly or annual

(B) Merit pay

(C) Traditional appraisal systems

(D) Quota system

(70)   In order to reduce the incidence of work-related stress among employees in an organization, management can employ an easy, cost-effective strategy that entails:

(A) Providing the fewest possible responsibilities to employees

(B) Making the work environment an open layout where every employee can easily hear and see what fellow employees are doing

(C) Emphasizing the need for employees to be competitive by adding to the incentives they already enjoy so that they can try to maximize productivity

(D) Planning ahead to minimize or entirely eliminate crises

(71) The Missouri Compromise:

(A) Was part of the land grab that eventually led to the Louisiana Purchase

(B) Accepted Maine as a free state in the Union and Missouri as a slave state

(C) Formalized Missouri as a state

(D) Made Missouri the very first state to receive amnesty following the end of the Civil War

(72)   How many members within the US House of Representatives are qualified to vote?

(A) 674

(B) 435

(C) 378

(D) 150

(73)   The US political party that started the system of using national conventions in the nomination process of presidential candidates was:

(A) The Federalist Party

(B) The Democratic Party

(C) The Republican Party

(D) The Anti-Masonic Party

(74)   One conqueror who became famous in the fifth century was referred to as "The Scourge of God." What was his real name?

(A) Attila the Hun

(B) William the Conqueror

(C) Hannibal

(D) Tsao Tsao

(75) Which of the people listed below did not live in the sixth century BC?

(A) Pythagoras

(B) Confucius

(C) Nero

(D) Buddha

(76) The _____ Empire ended after the Goth invasion that took place during the fifth century.

(A) Roman

(B) Ottoman

(C) Byzantine

(D) Qing

(77) In 1991, the _____ revolution caused Soviet troops to withdraw from Czechoslovakia.

(A) Cultural

(B) Red October

(C) Velvet

(D) Prague

(78) The leader famously known for crossing the Rubicon is:

(A) Augustus Caesar

(B) Alexander the Great

(C) Napoleon

(D) Julius Caesar

(79)   China's capital in 1928 was:

(A) Ghuang Zhou

(B) Nanjing

(C) Beijing

(D) Shanghai

(80)   If a government intervenes in a bid to correct an apparent failure within the market, this is said to be inefficient if:

(A) Its action causes businesses to close

(B) Anyone becomes the loser as a result

(C) The overall cost of implementing the action proves greater than the resulting benefit

(D) Its action leads to unemployment

(81) If you have a good known as X and another known as Y, and if X's price rises in tandem with Y's demand, X and Y are said to be:

(A) Normal goods

(B) Inferior goods

(C) Complements

(D) Substitutes

(82)   If you have a good known as X and another known as Y, and if X's price rises as Y's demand drops, X and Y are said to be:

(A) Normal goods

(B) Complements

(C) Substitutes

(D) Inferior goods

(83)   To the west of the Continental Divide is the state capital of:

(A) Salem

(B) Colombia

(C) Frankfurt

(D) Montgomery

(84)   The country sometimes referred to as the "Teardrop of India" and which was officially known as Ceylon in the past is:

(A) Nepal

(B) Bangladesh

(C) Nepal

(D) Sri Lanka

(85)   The tiniest independent country in the whole world with regard to its geographical area is:

(A) Monaco

(B) San Marino

(C) The Vatican

(D) Tuvalu

(868) The mountain considered the highest in the entire world when its measurement is taken right from the level of its own oceanic base is:

(A) Mauna Loa

(B) Mauna Kea

(C) Kohala

(D) Kilauea

(87)   Among the actions listed below, one does not always enhance competition among companies. Which one is it?

(A) The existence of several competitors whose strength is roughly the same

(B) High overhead costs

(C) Slow growth of industry

(D) Industry deregulation

(88)   To avoid high staff turnover when the industry is very competitive, a company should:

(A) Increase its recruitment efforts

(B) Reduce its expenditures on HR

(C) Introduce programs geared toward employee retention

(D) Enhance competitiveness within the workplace

(89)   One of the options below did not contribute to the prosperity of America during the 1950s.

(A) Increase in public expenditure

(B) The baby boomers era and increase in the number of suburbs

(C) Spending during the Cold War

(D) Introduction of computer technology

(90)   Which of the options listed below contributed to people's rapid shift to the suburbs?

(A) Hope of bigger, safer homes

(B) A more exciting lifestyle

(C) Integration of diverse races

(D) Rising prices within urban centers

(91) With regards to children, Dr. Spock told women to:

(A) Seek the advice of experts about raising children

(B) Be affectionate with their children and trust their personal instincts

(C) Make sure fathers play an equal role in raising the children

(D) Pursue goals beyond the home

(92) During the Space Race, the United States managed to _____ before the USSR.

(A) Put a man on Mars

(B) Put a man in space

(C) Put a man on the moon

(D) Put an unmanned satellite in space

(93) Rock 'n' roll and the Beat Generation had something in common. What was it?

(A) Resistance to conformity during the 1950s

(B) Being defined by music that was played long after they left the scene

(C) Being deeply nationalistic

(D) Their fight against racial discrimination

(94)   During his final formal address, President Eisenhower warned the people of America against:

(A) Proliferation of nuclear arms

(B) Communism

(C) The military industrial complex

(D) The resurgence of Nazism

(95)   President Kennedy's legislative efforts were continually blocked by the:

(A) Southern Democrats

(B) Senate Republicans

(C) Supreme Court

(D) State governors

(96)   The primary group involved in sit-ins, which entailed protesting against segregation within the Southern states, was composed of:

(A) Religious leaders of black descent

(B) Lawyers of black descent

(C) Liberal politicians

(D) Students of black descent

(97)   The sheriff who terrified Americans with his violent acts and whose brutality ended up winning sympathy for the ongoing civil rights movement was:

(A) Stokely Carmichael

(B) Eugene "Bull" Connor

(C) George Wallace

(D) Martin Luther King

(98)   The Cuban Missile Crisis resulted in _____, among other things.

(A) US President Kennedy and Soviet Union Prime Minister Nikita Khrushchev embarking on a series of meetings

(B) The Soviet Union building the Berlin Wall

(C) President Kennedy sending nuclear missiles into Turkey

(D) The Nuclear Test Ban Treaty being signed

(99)   According to President Johnson, _____ gave him leeway to escalate the Vietnam conflict.

(A) The Gulf of Tonkin Resolution

(B) Constitutional war powers

(C) Being commander in chief

(D) A declaration of war by Congress against Vietnam

(100) In the United States, The Weathermen were:

(A)A folk band that counted Bob Dylan as a member

(B)A violent student organization with political inclinations in the 1960s and 1970s

(C)A group of scientists that became prominent during the 1970s

(D) A group of literary experts that was linked to the Beats

(101) The issue that most significantly united the New Left during the late 1960s was:

(A)Women's rights

(B)Opposition to the war in Vietnam

(C)Civil rights

(D) Opposition against the abortion ban

(102) The "termination" approach to Native Americans by the US government argued for:

(A)Elimination of the reservations meant for Native Americans

(B)Termination of the immunity enjoyed by Native Americans against state laws

(C)Elimination of recognition of Native American tribes as legal entities

(D) Elimination of Native Americans' US citizenship

(103) The Marielitos were:

(A)People of Cuban origin who came to the United States in 1980

(B)American citizens born to workers of Hispanic origin

(C)People of Puerto Rican origin who settled in New York in the 1970s

(D) Illegal immigrants working for only part of the year

(104) Cesar Chavez is remembered for:

(A) Striving to defend the rights of minorities in the US Northeast

(B) Organizing Hispanic workers in the agricultural sector

(C) Being the first Hispanic to win a heavyweight boxing championship

(D) Being the first Hispanic Congressman

(105) The very first woman in America to be on the ticket of one of the dominant political parties during a presidential election was:

(A) Sarah Palin

(B) Sandra Day O'Connor

(C) Hillary Clinton

(D) Geraldine Ferrero

(106) The constitutional justification for the ruling in the Roe v. Wade case was:

(A) Right to privacy

(B) Protection of the rights of states

(C) Freedom of expression

(D) Religious freedom

(107) The reason Nixon could venture into China was:

(A) He was the only president who had the requisite interpersonal skills

(B) He could speak Chinese fluently

(C) He was the only one the Chinese could have welcomed

(D) He was known to be zealously against communism

(108) The reason for the plummeting of President's Ford's popularity was:

(A) His decision to run for reelection

(B) Nothing; he was unpopular all through his term

(C) His decision to pardon Richard Nixon

(D) His decision to increase taxes

(109) By the time President Jimmy Carter's term in office came to an end, the US economy:

(A) Had no unemployment and growth was steady

(B) Had high growth and low inflation

(C) Was marked by high levels of unemployment and mild deflation

(D) Had record-high interest and inflation rates

(110) Ronald Reagan was the most popular candidate in 1984's presidential race. He won in all the US states, apart from:

(A) Minnesota

(B) New York

(C) Massachusetts

(D) California

(111)   Supply-side economics is based on the theory that:

(A) Military spending will succeed in spurring the economy

(B) Reducing taxes will succeed in spurring the economy

(C) Government spending will succeed in spurring the economy

(D) Giving subsidies to oil suppliers will succeed in spurring the economy

(112)   One achievement attributed to President Bill Clinton is:

(A) Allowing gay soldiers to be open about their sexuality while serving in the military

(B) Solving the conflict between Israel and Palestine

(C) Enacting universal health care

(D) Balancing the US federal budget

(113)   All options listed below except one accurately explain changes in the American economy during the late 1980s and 1990s. Which option does not explain the changes?

(A) The degree of wealth inequality rose

(B) For the first time in a century, America experienced its lowest rate of poverty

(C) The significance of manufacturing decreased

(D) There was a rise in the number of families with multiple incomes

(114)   At the end of the 20th century, some major achievements in the field of technology occurred. Which of the choices listed below does not constitute one of those achievements?

(A) Development in Texas of the Superconducting Super Collider

(B) Expansive increase in cell-phone networks

(C) Development of the internet

(D) Completion of the Human Genome Project

(115)   The strong US political movement that supports candidates who are anti-abortion is:

(A) The evangelical movement

(B) The neocon movement

(C) The right-to-life movement

(D) The moral majority

(116)   Which of the options listed below does not have a record of being opposed to globalization?

(A) Labor activists

(B) The International Monetary Fund

(C) Human rights activists

(D) Environmentalists

(117)   The longest war in US history was:

(A) World War II

(B) The Afghanistan War

(C) The Vietnam War

(D) World War I

(118)   The period when the United States experienced the highest level of unemployment was:

(A) The Great Depression

(B) Soon after the end of the American Civil War

(C) During the mid-1800s

(D) Soon after the 2008 financial collapse

(119)   With the knowledge you have of the region's geography, which of the choices below would you say was a key activity that was economically affected by Israel's victory in 1967's Six-Day War?

(A) Export of agricultural products from the Sinai Peninsula

(B) The Dead Sea shipping trade

(C) Industrial production within the Gaza Strip

(D) Transportation of products via the Suez Canal

(120) Which option below best explains the difference in urbanization between Germany and Portugal?

(A) Portugal is essentially isolated from other parts of Europe

(B) The importance of agriculture in Germany is minimal

(C) Portugal has not yet joined the European Union

(D) Germany happens to be in the middle of Europe's industrial belt

(121) _____ imports most of the wheat consumed in the country.

(A) Russia

(B) France

(C) Japan

(D) Australia

(122) Which of the methods listed below most accurately depicts the level of desertification within a given region?

(A) Seismic readings

(B) Contour maps

(C) Satellite imagery

(D) Long-range weather forecasts

(123) Of the countries listed below, _____ is the one with the greatest trade with the United States in regards to volume and value.

(A) Germany

(B) Japan

(C) Canada

(D) Great Britain

(124) In America, the Midwest's fertile soil is a result of:

(A) Glaciers

(B) Sandstones that were eroded

(C) Decayed organic material

(D) Volcanic activity

(125) Which of the statements listed below is true of developing countries' economies?

(A) The goods they export are mainly raw agricultural materials

(B) They normally have a highly developed manufacturing sector

(C) The goods they import are mostly confined to those manufactured

(D) They normally produce goods that are of a highly technological nature

(126)   Women are more adversely affected by desertification in East African countries than men because:

(A) The countries have a bigger population of women than men

(B) Women are the ones mainly in charge of gathering wood for fuel and water for domestic use

(C) Women generally use much more water than men do

(D) The size of families generally increases when there is a drought

(127)   The forces of gravity, wind, ice and water have an effect on the general natural environment because:

(A) They highly contribute to erosion

(B) They are known to contribute to continental drift

(C) They highly contribute to seismic activity

(D) They are a great influence to the development of human settlements

(128)   There are times when El Niño, the warm ocean current, is replaced by the cooler Peru current. This happens along the Peruvian coastline, and as a result, anchovies that seabirds rely on for food decrease. Owing to that shortage of birds, there is a drop in the number of birds left to roost along the Peruvian coastal islands. In the country of Peru, such developments negatively affect the:

(A) Coastal weather that is normally warm

(B) Money normally earned through tourism along the beaches

(C) Ships' capacity to dock within the local ports

(D) Quantities of anchovies exported

(129)   One set of countries in a zone with a tropical climate is:

(A) New Zealand, Bolivia and Syria

(B) Vietnam, Turkey and Portugal

(C) Uganda, Indonesia and Panama

(D) Japan, Morocco and Uruguay

(130) _____ in Canada is inaccessible using any of the main highways.

(A) The area of Northwest Territories

(B) The Yukon Territory

(C) New Brunswick

(D) Quebec

(131)   The physical feature separating Siberia from European Russia is:

(A) The Ural Mountains

(B) The Volga River

(C) The Caspian Sea

(D) The Central Siberian Plateau

(132)   The reason that a good number of people living in the Caribbean have West African roots is that:

(A) They came to partake of economic opportunities in the Caribbean

(B) West Africans were taken as slaves to work on agricultural plantations

(C) Urbanization in the region has been rapid

(D) They were persecuted in their country of origin

(133) During the last half century, _____ have/has affected the growth of US suburbs.

(A) Automobiles

(B) Electricity

(C) Computers

(D) High-speed rail transport

(134) The formation of fossil fuels like coal or oil is due to:

(A) Processes of a geological nature that transform organic matter into compost

(B) The breaking down of big rocks into tiny particles

(C) Processes of an organic nature that cause animal tissue fossilization

(D) The rapid decay of animal bones

(135) The best way to explain diffusion is to note that crops once farmed mainly in the Americas now:

(A) Are grown in all regions of the world

(B) Are not grown anymore in America

(C) Can be found only within the Northern Hemisphere

(D) Are now found only in regions where there is high productivity

(136)   To the south of latitude 60°, one can generally find:

(A) Floating icebergs

(B) Inuit settlements

(C) Lack of insect life and animal life in general

(D) Commercial shipping lanes

(137)   In general, most people today emigrate from their home countries:

(A) In search of better economic opportunities

(B) In search of places with better climatic conditions

(C) In search of places with more religious freedom

(D) After being expelled from their home countries

(138)   When a megalopolis develops, it exemplifies:

(A) Great regional planning

(B) Urbanization

(C) Gentrification

(D) Deforestation

(139)   The reason the world's major oil-producing countries joined to form OPEC was that:

(A) They wanted to have greater control of the oil market and prices

(B) They wanted to enhance the production of fossil fuels while improving oil quality

(C) They wanted to enhance communication among developing countries and improve transportation networks

(D) They wanted to limit the access other countries had to solar energy

(140) The religion followed by most people in India is:

(A) Christianity

(B) Buddhism

(C) Confucianism

(D) Hinduism

(141) The term "Corn Belt" is used for a region whose basis of definition is its:

(A) Political affiliation

(B) Major economic activity

(C) Population

(D) Transportation network

(142) Rising population has adversely affected coral reefs in some parts of the world, and one place that faces the greatest threat is:

(A) The Persian Gulf, close to Iran and Saudi Arabia

(B) South America, close to Argentina and Brazil

(C) Southeast Asia, close to Indonesia and the Philippines

(D) The western part of Africa, close to the Ivory Coast and Liberia

(143) Japan is most likely to import its forest products from:

(A) The United States

(B) South Korea

(C) Germany

(D) Australia

(144)   The least populated US region is:

(A) The Southwest

(B) The Northeast

(C) The Rocky Mountains

(D) The Pacific

(145)   A city's central area is likely to have:

(A) Family homes

(B) Steel factories

(C) Office high-rises

(D) Car dealerships

(146)   Which option below is most likely to be found where land is level?

(A) An amusement park, a quarry and a ski resort

(B) A hydroelectric plant, a reservoir and a national park

(C) An orchard, a mine and a coffee farm

(D) A railroad, an airport and a city

(147)   The reason the city of New York has residents from different parts of the world and public-school students who speak a wide range of languages is that:

(A) New York offers a minimum wage that is higher than other places in the United States

(B) New York is the location of the UN headquarters

(C) New York is a port through which people access the United States from elsewhere in the world

(D) New York's system of transportation is efficient

(148)   Before railroads were built in the United States, _____ were most commonly used to transport commercial items like timber and coal during the mid-19th century.

(A) Canals and rivers

(B) Ox-driven carts and Conestoga wagons

(C) Mule trains and pack horses

(D) Freeways and turnpikes

(149)   What do areas like the central United States and Argentina's Pampas, as well as countries like Ukraine, Canada and the south central area of Australia, have in common that makes them ideal for wheat production?

(A) They are highland areas

(B) Their climates are rainy and damp

(C) They are all plains

(D) They are all close to coastlines

(150) Sometimes you can locate snowy areas within an equatorial region when:

(A) It is winter

(B) The area is below sea level

(C) The area is at a high elevation

(D) The area is at a high latitude

(151) The equator runs across which set of countries listed below?

(A) Paraguay, Papua New Guinea and Zimbabwe

(B) Pakistan, Mexico and Nigeria

(C) The Philippines, Iceland and Angola

(D) Ecuador, Kenya and Gabon

(152) Traveling by road to Rome from Paris, one passes a major physical barrier. That is:

(A) The Rhone River

(B) The Alps

(C) The Massif Central

(D) The Mediterranean

(153) Which of the states listed below shares a similar climate with Alice Springs in Australia?

(A) Illinois

(B) Washington

(C) Florida

(D) Arizona

(154) In Ireland, land is mainly used for:

(A) Mixed farming–growing crops and rearing animals

(B) Manufacturing industries and commerce

(C) Big ranches

(D) Forestry

(155) The pair of natural features that form a big part of Chile's border are:

(A) The Atacama Desert and Patagonia

(B) The Andes Mountains and the Pacific Ocean

(C) The Strait of Magellan and the Pampas

(D) The Amazon River basin and Lake Titicaca

(156) Japan enjoys the best balance of trade with:

(A) Indonesia

(B) Taiwan

(C) The United States

(D) China

(157)   In the United States, the major natural vegetation in areas that now produce corn used to be:

(A) Forests of broadleaf trees and grasslands

(B) Forests of needleleaf trees

(C) Steppes

(D) Tropical rainforests

(158)   There is usually conflict between consumers' preference for manufactured products and energy and:

(A) Global trade

(B) Clean environment

(C) Improved living standards

(D) Technological advancements

(159)   It is true to say that in the American Southwest:

(A) The manufacturing sector has thrived due to the area's proximity to Mexico

(B) Dry conditions cause water to become a fundamental issue for the public

(C) Travel is difficult owing to the alternating features of sand dunes and thick shrubbery

(D) A good many people depend on solar energy for domestic use courtesy of the fair weather

(160) Trade barriers among _____ were reduced by NAFTA.

(A) The United States, Japan and Mexico

(B) The United States, France and Germany

(C) The United States, Brazil and Chile

(D) The United States, Canada and Mexico

(161)   In order to be able to predict the area with the most likelihood of acid rain falling, a scientist would very likely study:

(A) Where treatment plants for sewage are located

(B) Atomic structures of oxygen, nitrogen and sulfur

(C) Wind patterns that normally prevail over areas where significant manufacturing takes place

(D) Transportation systems that mainly serve big cities and their suburbs

(162)   Quebec is accepted as one of the world's cultural regions because of its:

(A) Economy

(B) Landforms

(C) Language

(D) Climate

(163) Advancements in communication that made it easy to convey messages across the globe in seconds involved:

(A) High-resolution TV signals

(B) Satellites used by telecommunications networks

(C) Postal service ZIP codes as well as high-speed sorting machines

(D) Telephone companies' area codes

(164) Pittsburgh became a significant center of steel production owing to:

(A) The city's close proximity to Canada's steel markets

(B) The city's close proximity to deposits of coal and iron

(C) The availability of a massive skilled workforce

(D) The city's favorable climate that enabled production of steel all year round

(165) _____ is likely to succeed in giving people a sense of cultural unity.

(A) Economic advancement

(B) Use of a common language

(C) Having a landscape that is diverse

(D) Rural-urban migration

(166)   On the western side of Europe, forests have mainly developed in areas of high elevation because:

(A) For trees to grow well, they need cool temperatures

(B) Trees have been planted by timber companies along the slopes of hills

(C) Trees generally do best on steep slopes

(D) All lowlands were cleared by people for farming

(167)   The Great Lakes were created because of:

(A) The effect of mountain runoffs

(B) What the glaciers did

(C) The effect of plate tectonic movements

(D) Dam construction

(168)   There are times when El Niño, the warm ocean current, is replaced by the cooler Peru current. This happens along the Peruvian coastline, and as a result, anchovies that seabirds rely on for food decrease. Owing to that shortage of birds, there is a drop in the number of birds left to roost along the Peruvian coastal islands.

This passage tells of the effect El Niño has on the _____ of Peru.

(A) Wind currents

(B) Coastal erosion

(C) Ecosystem

(D) Weather

(169) One major reason countries choose to become members of international bodies such as the UN is that:

(A) The organization forces individual countries to become members

(B) Many of the problems the world faces affect more than a single country

(C) If a country fails to join, it normally loses its independence

(D) The majority of citizens prefer their respective countries to become members of as many international organizations as possible

(170) The country of Switzerland is situated within a mountain range called:

(A) The Alps

(B) The Pyrenees

(C) The Andes

(D) The Urals

(171) _____ follow a profession that requires them to live in many places.

(A) Technicians in oil refineries

(B) Nurses

(C) Cattle ranchers

(D) Miners

(172)   Most of the towns in ancient Greece were developed on hilltops mainly because:

(A) In the early days, Greeks did not depend on farming for their food

(B) Water was more readily available on hilltops than in low-lying lands

(C) It was easier to defend a town on a hilltop than one in a low-lying area

(D) Temperatures got warmer as one got to more elevated areas

(173)   Disposal of detergents after use has been found to destabilize _____ natural balance.

(A) Climatic conditions'

(B) Ocean currents'

(C) The atmosphere's

(D) Lakes' and streams'

(174)   _____ contributes greatly to the greenhouse effect.

(A) Water pollution

(B) Burning of fuels (e.g., gas, oil and coal)

(C) Erosion of soil

(D) Not using crop rotation

(175)   Which of the countries listed below is farthest south?

(A) Zaire

(B) South Africa

(C) New Zealand

(D) Uruguay

(176)   In the late 1800s, one factor that contributed greatly to the expansion of human settlements westwards was:

(A) The construction of canals

(B) The construction of the railway

(C) Shipbuilding

(D) The construction of highways

(177)   Based on your geographical knowledge, which statement below is most likely to be true?

(A) Ships heading to South America from New York have to pass through the Panama Canal

(B) If ships did not use the Panama Canal when coming from San Francisco, the only other route to get to New York would be 8,370 km long

(C) If ships did not use the Panama Canal when coming from San Francisco, the only other route to get to New York would be 13,000 miles long

(D) It is mandatory for ships entering South America from San Francisco to use the Panama Canal

(178)   Among the cities listed below, which one rates highest in terms of manufacturing and trade?

(A) Kinshasa in Congo

(B) Lusaka in Zambia

(C) Tunis in Tunisia

(D) Luanda in Angola

(179)   The smallest ocean in the world is:

(A) The Antarctic

(B) The Arctic

(C) The Indian Ocean

(D) The Atlantic

(180)   The state of Florida is a good example of:

(A) A plateau

(B) An isthmus

(C) A peninsula

(D) An island

(181)   Why did early peoples often settle within river valleys?

(A) It was easier for them to defend their settlements from attacks than if they lived on higher grounds

(B) In river valleys they were safer from wild animals

(C) River valleys were cooler than areas at a higher elevation

(D) The soil in the river valleys was rich because of the deposits that came with floodwaters

(182)   One major reason US cities began to build skyscrapers was:

(A) So that residents could be protected from crime happening in the streets

(B) Construction companies felt residents would feel like they occupied single-family housing units

(C) Land was more intensively and efficiently utilized

(D) Residents were able to form close communities

(183)   Among the continents listed below, _____ is in the lead with respect to manufacturing and trade.

(A) South America

(B) Europe

(C) Australia

(D) Africa

(184)   The region highest in elevation in the continent of Africa is:

(A) The northern coast

(B) The southwestern side

(C) The western coast

(D) The eastern coast

(185) Which of these is a capital city on the African continent?

(A) Luanda in Angola

(B) Kananga in the DRC

(C) Durban in South Africa

(D) Bulawayo in Zimbabwe

(186) Which of the options below has the highest elevation?

(A) Lake Titicaca

(B) Parana River

(C) Gran Chaco

(D) Brazilian Highlands

(187) The equator runs across which of the countries below?

(A) India

(B) Bolivia

(C) Australia

(D) Indonesia

(188) Which step comes first in the process of strategic management?

(A) Strategic analysis

(B) Strategy formulation

(C) Strategic posturing

(D) Implementation of strategy

(189) From the options provided below, choose the one with people who ought to be involved when strategies are being implemented.

(A) All heads of divisions

(B) The main shareholders

(C) The CEO as well as the entire board of directors

(D) All the people mentioned in options (A) to (C)

(190) Lucy traveled from New York to Greece in December 2001 and found a nice blouse that cost 6,274 drachmas. As per the prevailing exchange rate, one dollar was equivalent to 200.5 drachmas. What was the price of the blouse in US dollars?

(A) $125.80

(B) $31.29

(C) $12.60

(D) $33.45

(191) Chef Abdi has a recipe that uses three cups of wheat flour, which is a mixture of both white and brown flour. Three-eighths of the three cups constitutes the white flour. How many cups of brown flour does Abdi need?

(A) 1.125 cups

(B) 1.875 cups

(C) 2.375 cups

(D) 2.625 cups

(192) Mary lives 6½ km from the school library. She is able to walk a third of the way without taking a rest. What is the distance she must still cover after resting?

(A) 5.83 km

(B) 4 km

(C) 4.33 km

(D) 2.16 km

(193) One-fourth of all cars sold by a local dealership are high-end luxury models. The dealership sold 360 cars from that category last year. What is the total number of cars the dealership sold last year?

(A) 3,600 cars

(B) 90 cars

(C) 1,440 cars

(D) 250 cars

(194) The number of people who fit in eight subway cars while seated is 400. How many people would fit in five subway cars while seated?

(A) 350

(B) 250

(C) 300

(D) 200

(195) Jepkosgei ran half a mile within four minutes. If she runs at the same rate, how far will she have run in 15 minutes?

(A) 1.875 miles

(B) 4 miles

(C) 60 miles

(D) 30 miles

(196) If you have a rope 10 feet long and you want to cut it into 8-inch-long segments, how many of those pieces will you have?

(A) 1 piece

(B) 8 pieces

(C) 15 pieces

(D) 40 pieces

(197) A reputable restaurant pays a tip of 15% on the bill after 6% tax has been charged. If the bill before tax and tip totals $38.40, what is the amount of the tip in dollars?

(A) $6.10

(B) $2.30

(C) $5.15

(D) $5.76

(198) For a certain company, cab charges for the initial mile total $3, and for every additional half mile the charge is $1. If Asha takes a cab ride for 10 miles, how much is she supposed to pay?

(A) $13

(B) $10

(C) $12

(D) $21

(199) An overseas automobile manufacturer pays $3 in shipping charges for every 1 kilogram of automobile parts sent to the United States. If the cargo sent weighs 200 pounds, how much should the manufacturer pay when rounded to the nearest dollar? Take the ratio of pound to kilogram to be 1:0.455.

(A) $152

(B) $60

(C) $132

(D) $273

(200) John spent $25 after dining in a city restaurant. He noted that the bill before tip was $21. Roughly what percentage tip did John leave?

(A) 25%

(B) 19%

(C) 16%

(D) 21%

Test 1: Answers & Explanations

(1) As a member of a management team that seeks to enhance its effectiveness and forge a great relationship with its employees while also trying to optimize the performance of the organization, you could make use of:

Correct answer is: (B) Upward feedback

Using upward feedback, employees have a chance to give feedback to their managers, telling them what they think ought to be done to improve service delivery and make management more effective. Overall, lower-ranking employees have an opportunity to provide information that can influence organizational policies.

(2) If the US Bureau of Labor Statistics decides to hire someone who has no disability even when a more qualified individual who uses a wheelchair also applied for the job, the bureau will have violated the:

The correct answer is: (A) Rehabilitation Act of 1973

The Rehabilitation Act of 1973, together with the Americans with Disabilities Act (ADA) of 1990, prohibits anyone from discriminating against people with any form of disability. In fact, the US federal government's hiring criteria are structured to best accommodate people with disabilities. It is important to note that the ADA is applicable to the private sector as well, not just to government institutions.

(3) An employer can legally ask a pregnant woman to:

The correct answer is: (B) Produce medical evidence showing that the pregnancy is making her incapable of working, thus causing her to require leave

Pregnant women in the United States are protected under the Pregnancy Discrimination Act as well as the Civil Rights of 1964, which requires employers to extend to pregnant women all the protections given to other employees, and to consider complications arising from pregnancy just like any other disability.

Nevertheless, employers are allowed to request medical documentation showing the extent of the disability just the same way that this would be required of people with different disabilities. Employers may not require workers to take leave due to pregnancy. In fact, pregnant women are permitted to work as long as they can before taking leave. It is illegal to allocate duties or workstations to pregnant women on the basis of what clients or other members of the public think.

(4) Per Title VII of the Civil Rights Act of 1964, a US employer can be sued if:

The correct answer is: (D) All of the above situations can lead to a legal suit

All three options can lead to a legal suit against the employer. Economic injury does not need to be proven for a sexual harassment suit.

(5) Any time a manager gets personally involved in order to motivate employees, there is a risk to employees:

The correct answer is: (A) Whose self-esteem is low and who are unable to meet high performance expectations

When a manager is personally involved in the work being done, employees are likely to be motivated to perform at their best and to commit fully to the success of the project. The result is likely to be high-quality performance that would probably not have been attained if the manager had not been personally involved. Incidentally, employees whose self-esteem is low require the guidance and support of management in order to enhance their self-confidence and be in a position to create higher goals. When it comes to employees committing verbally to great performance, it means a lot as far as the success of the project is concerned, and the same case applies to the commitments employees make in a group set-up. These two have a way of leading to the success of the project or task involved.

(6) Performance management can be replaced by another method referred to as:

The correct answer is: (B) A traditional appraisal system

The traditional appraisal system is a good replacement for performance management, as its main focus encompasses all employees, beginning with new hires and those leaving the organization.

(7) According to the FSLA, any employee who is exempt and earns $28.50 an hour while working 45 hours a week should receive a paycheck amounting to:

The correct answer is: (A) $1,282.50

Employees who are defined as being exempt as far as the Fair Labor Standard Act (FLSA) is concerned are not eligible for overtime and are paid on an hourly basis.

(8) The reason employers are expected to fill in form I-9 for every employee is to verify:

The correct answer is: (A) That the person is eligible to work in the United States

The I-9 form has been used in the United States since 1986, and it serves to show the federal government that all employees working in the country are doing so legally, whether they are US citizens or not. It requires that details such as a driver's license, Social Security card, visa and the like be submitted as proof that an employee is really eligible for employment in the United States

(9) It is incumbent upon the manager to see to it that every employee is given a job description that is clear and accurate. If this does not happen, the employer could be liable for:

The correct answer is: (B) Legal suits associated with violating the ADA

If an employer uses a job description that is not clear, it is easy to be sued for matters associated with the employee's performance in that job, as well as issues relating to termination of that employee's services. Someone could sue the employer for discrimination under the ADA.

(10)There is sometimes some vagueness when it comes to employee appraisals. A good way to remedy this is by supplementing the standard company forms with:

The correct answer is: (C) Written comments with more clearly explained rating scales

Managers conducting appraisals should refrain from using forms that are not authorized by the company's legal counsel and human resources department, even when those conventional forms contain details that are a little vague. They should also refrain from relying on verbal communication between them and the employee being appraised, and instead supplement the standard forms with explanations and remarks in written form.

(11) Skewing appraisals positively just because employees are performing well in some areas should be avoided. This tendency is referred to as:

The correct answer is: (C) Halo effect

It is best for managers to avoid the halo effect when carrying out a positive evaluation of employees based on performance that is limited to just a few areas or departments.

(12)During the process of evaluation or appraisal, which of the areas listed below would be considered soft in regard to employees being likely to feel personally offended?

The correct answer is: (C) Teamwork

Normally, employees respond in a positive way when evaluations are carried out in a black-and-white manner, such as discussing sales-revenue figures. This type of evidence is hard to dispute. Whereas such evidence may be a source of disappointment for employees and may cause all manner of excuses to be made, it is unlikely that an employee will feel he or she is being unfairly blamed.

Areas with unclear definition are referred to as "soft areas," and when criticism is within those areas, employees are likely to take it as blame directed at them personally.

(13)If a manager focuses on _____, he or she is very likely to successfully motivate employees in the long-term.

The correct answer is: (C) Understanding both the goals and interests of employees

Trying to motivate employees through financial benefits has a short-term effect. Incentives of a financial nature cannot sustain motivation on a long-term basis. For long-term employee motivation, it is important to create a working environment that is sensitive to employees' interests. That kind of environment will motivate employees to pursue their goals and excel.

(14) Managers making use of the Pygmalion Effect often succeed in getting employees to perform well by:

The correct answer is: (A) Showing them they are very capable of achieving set goals

The Pygmalion Effect involves the belief that if you raise the standards and expectations for employees, they tend to produce better results and generally perform better than before.

(15) On the basis of Maslow's Hierarchy of Needs, people attach more importance or put more emphasis upon:

The correct answer is: (C) Needs of a physiological nature

Maslow believed that, while trying to understand how human beings are motivated, it is imperative to view the hierarchy within which certain required needs have to be fulfilled. Before they fulfill higher needs, such as education, people need to have fulfilled lower needs that are of a physiological nature, such as having access to food, water and shelter.

(16) Supervising employee productivity and how they perform activities on a daily basis is the generally accepted role of management, but there needs to be a balance because micromanaging employees can often end up:

The correct answer is: (B) Stifling inventiveness

The tendency to micromanage people could be taken to mean that you as the employer or manager have no confidence or trust in the ability of the employees to perform on their own. This could then lead to resentment from employees and cause their morale to drop. This habit also has the potential to inhibit employees' creativity and resourcefulness while also curtailing initiative.

(17) A person who actively listens manifests all traits listed below except:

The correct answer is: (A) Often completing other people's sentences

People who are active listeners do a lot more listening than talking. They allow other people room to express themselves and to complete the thoughts and ideas that they have.

(18) Regarding employees' personal lives, managers should:

The correct answer is: (A) Take an interest, and then show their concern where necessary while empathizing with the employees

It is not practical to ignore your employees' personal lives if you are a good manager because personal problems have a way of impacting people's capacity to work. Managers ought to be concerned about things that affect employees at a personal level. They should be empathetic and ensure affected employees get help without prying into a person's private life. Managers trying to assist employees with personal challenges should use a tone consistent with a manager/employee relationship.

(19) Going by the Civil Rights Act's Title VII, it is illegal for an employer to inhibit the religious practice of any employee when at the workplace unless:

The correct answer is: (B) The employee's religious practice makes the work environment unsafe

This particular part of the law prohibits employers from discriminating against any employee based on their religion in the process of hiring and during employment unless there is good reason for the employer to believe accommodation of such religious practices has the potential to introduce unnecessary difficulties for the employer or other people working in the organization and the employer can demonstrate this fact. Other exemptions include the religious belief or practice violating any regulation or law or creating an unsafe work environment.

(20)   Suppose you have recently established a management job that has more than 500 employees, and you find out that there are some practices in your company that are not compliant with the Equal Pay Act of 1963 and all other amendments associated with it. You could take all the steps listed below in order to remedy the situation except:

The correct answer is: (C) Reduce the pay for employees earning unduly higher wages than others of a different gender doing similar jobs while trying to equalize employees' remuneration

The Equal Pay Act of 1963 explicitly prohibits reduction of an employee's wage in order to become compliant with a regulation or law.

(21) When as a manager you want to reduce stress associated with work in your workforce, you can use a cost-effective and easy-to-follow strategy, which entails:

The correct answer is: (B) Practicing a strategy of planning ahead that reduces the need to manage a crisis

Options (A), (C) and (D) are bound to raise employees' level of stress. An office with an open layout sometimes becomes very noisy and distracting. As such, employees are unable to complete tasks as required, which can be a source of stress.

Giving employees the least responsibilities possible can give them a feeling of insecurity, making them fear for their current jobs. At the same time, competition in excess can be stressful to employees.

(22)   When it comes to designing jobs, both managers and employees can reduce stress by doing all of the following things except:

The correct answer is: (C) Establishing working hours that lead to the highest level of profits for the company

The way working hours and shifts are designed should consider employees' health and comfort before considering business profitability.

(23)   When as an employer you involve different people in an employee evaluation, such as fellow coworkers, supervisors or customers, such a process is referred to as:

The correct answer is: (A) 360° feedback

The 360° feedback evaluation is based on the assumption that you can evaluate an employee best when you listen to the perspectives of different parties who have interacted with the employee and have knowledge of them within the work environment.

(24)   When it is time to interview a person for a job, aptitude tests are often carried out in the early stages of the process to evaluate:

The correct answer is: (D) The candidate's general capacity to reason and write well

Normally, aptitude tests are given in the early stages of the interview to assess the candidate's overall skills in areas of a basic nature, like math and reasoning as well as verbal and written communication.

(25)   You are invited to be part of an ad hoc committee formed to see what changes are appropriate for the company's benefits package. Such a committee very likely will:

The correct answer is: (A) Meet on a regular basis until the completion of the necessary changes

Going by the term "ad hoc," which means "set for a specified purpose," the committee will perform a specific task and will be disbanded after completion of that job. The committee is unlikely to be able to complete its work in a single sitting or a single meeting as suggested in option (B). Also, the issue of permanence as suggested in option (C) is unlikely. As for option (D), it is incorrect because one reason such ad hoc committees are formed is to make the board's burden lighter.

(26)   When two employees clash during meetings and make their colleagues uncomfortable, what is the best action to take?

The correct answer is: (B) Counsel the clashing employees on better ways of working together and keep monitoring their progress going forward

The most logical way to solve the problem is to mediate while trying to find practical solutions and then keep tabs on the situation to ensure things are getting better.

Firing one of the clashing employees is unlikely to solve the problem, as you may not have sufficient proof that the particular employee was the real cause of the problem. As for reassigning the employees to separate areas of work, this might not be helpful and could instead send a negative message to other employees about how conflicts should be handled. It might even demoralize them, especially if you remove someone they like working with.

(27)   Researchers in the field of psychology, including Abraham Maslow and Kurt Goldstein, have explored the theory of self-actualization. Choose the option below that best supports this theory.

The correct answer is: (B) An employee works consistently for one company for 30 years, during which he rises in rank from an office clerk to the position of regional vice-president

Proponents of the theory of self-actualization believe that when it comes to human beings, the upward rise to the highest point of their capabilities is instinctive.

(28)   The discipline in which people learn about human behavior within the workplace, both as individuals and as groups, is commonly referred to as:

The correct answer is: (A) Organizational or industrial psychology

Industrial or organizational psychology is sometimes simply referred to as I-O psychology. It focuses on how to increase productivity at work by addressing the welfare of employees at a physical and mental level. This discipline employs different principles and theories in psychology to help organizations improve.

(29)   Under the Civil Rights Act's Title IV, any company whose practice of hiring employees includes _____ violates the law.

The correct answer is: (C) Coding résumés/applications according to candidates' race or gender

The act of coding candidates' résumés or applications by gender, religion, national origin or any of the other categories that are protected by law can easily be construed to mean you support discriminatory tendencies in your hiring process.

(30)   There are different ways of keeping employees motivated. Among them are two significant categories, namely factors of hygiene and motivators. Identify the choice below that falls under the category of motivators: one that cannot succeed unless needs of a basic nature or factors of hygiene are fulfilled.

The correct answer is: (B) Advancement

Option (A) is the best answer because all the other options have items that represent basic needs as far as an employee is concerned, including salary, vacation and security.

These are needs that are not expected to be necessarily motivating once they are met, but if the employer does not fulfill them, the employees will not be motivated to work. Advancement is not considered a basic need, but it is good at motivating employees once they are provided for.

(31) Some managers believe it is possible to divide management styles into two groups, namely Theory X and Theory Y. The latter is said to be motivating and emphasizes ordinary collaboration between managers and their staff, while welcoming input and feedback from employees for the sake of making decisions. A manager of this type is very likely:

The correct answer is: (B) To keep rotating chairmanship of the company's regular staff meetings

Managers who follow Theory X are known to issue commands from afar and make most of their decisions on their own without involving the employees in any significant way or getting any input from them. Such managers consider subordinate staff not to have any ambition or drive. Managers under Theory Y liaise with their staff as they go through the decision-making process, welcome input from them and even guide those who require assistance in order to succeed. These managers and their juniors have a team spirit as they carry out their obligations.

(32)   Assume there is a group of employees working for you as a team on a project estimated to take six months. When you decide you need to reinforce ownership of team member tasks, the best way to go about it is:

The correct answer is: (B) To delegate fresh tasks to individual members of the team in order to differentiate their experience

When you delegate work to your team or individuals, you remain hands-off as far as work completion is concerned. Often you need to have someone else oversee the day-to-day tasks, such as an advisor or a coach.

(33)   There are some situations that qualify an employee for the Family and Medical Leave Act (FMLA). Which of the options below is such a situation?

The correct answer is: (D) Aisha has been working for close to one year as manager of a national restaurant chain that has 10 branches within a 50-mile radius. She has recently adopted a child and has consequently requested three weeks of leave.

According to the FMLA, after childbirth, adoption or if a member of the employee's nuclear family is seriously ill or an employee is ill, he or she can take up to 12 weeks of unpaid leave if the company he or she is working for has over 50 employees who are within 75 miles from the workstation.

(34) All of the options below except one are in compliance with the Americans with Disabilities Act (ADA). Which is the exception?

The correct answer is: (C) Asking a candidate to clarify his or her physical limitations due to a visible physical disability

According to the ADA, employers should accommodate employees and job applicants with various disabilities, but they are not obliged to retain or employ those who put undue difficulties on the business, such as those who will cause production to drop.

Medical examinations that are specific to given jobs are permitted if all applicants are required to go through them.

As for drug screening, this is not taken as a medical examination. So any applicant, whether disabled or not, can be drug tested without going against the ADA. Employers are not permitted to inquire about a candidate's disability, whether known or unknown, but they can inquire about the candidate's capacity to carry out the requirements of a particular job.

(35)   According to the 1978 Civil Service Reform Act, government agencies that are establishing merit pay systems should take into account all of the options listed below except:

The correct answer is: (D) A person's marital status

It is explicitly indicated in the act that an employer cannot consider a person's race, marital status, age or religion when determining his or her pay scale.

(36)   Any manager in a given government agency is failing to comply with the 1978 Civil Service Reform Act if he or she designs a system of appraisal for an employee that:

The correct answer is: (B) Calls for immediate termination of employees rated poorly during evaluation

The Civil Service Reform Act of 1978 has a stipulation that any employee whose evaluation results are poor must be accorded a chance to improve his or her performance. That same law also indicates that an employee should be assessed regularly for performance, even as it encourages the participation of employees in designing the evaluation process.

(37)   Which of the management styles listed below is very good for managing highly trained professionals who are very creative and highly self-motivated:

The correct answer is: (A) Laissez-faire

Laissez-faire is the hands-off management approach. It can work quite well with the category of employees described in the question: highly trained professionals who are creative and greatly motivated. Nevertheless, it is important to note that though this approach works impressively well, it should not happen by chance just because of poor management. It should be a deliberate move by the person in charge. The reason is that the kind of employees who fall under this category are unlikely to tolerate any autocratic management approach that has the potential to curtail decision-making or other similar freedoms. In fact, these are the kinds of employees who do not like management styles that are in any way paternalistic, even if the intentions are good.

(38)   When you want to assess a job applicant for _____, you might ask a question such as, "Can you remember a colleague in your last place of work who you found difficult to work with, and what can you tell me about how you coped with that challenge?"

The correct answer is: (A) How well he or she handles stressful situations

This type of question is meant to make the applicant analyze a situation in the past that caused him or her stress. At the same time, this kind of question is not exactly easy, so it is bound to put some level of strain on the candidate. This gives the interviewer or the interviewing panel a chance to see firsthand how the job applicant responds to stress, even as they listen to the candidate's version of a past stressful situation.

(39)   The management team has decided to implement a Continuous Improvement Plan (CIP), the kind that Edward Deming suggested is best to help a department fulfill long-term goals. On the basis of the CIP, you will likely:

The correct answer is: (B) Create a document that specifies the actions you want done

A Continuous Improvement Plan is very specific and involves writing down goal plans and the actions you plan on undertaking. It also includes feedback on a regular basis, close monitoring and appraisal, as well as modification. The CIP also emphasizes quality. In brief, the model by Deming is to plan, then do and thereafter check and act.

(40)   If you decide against hiring a candidate on the grounds that he or she is limited in English language proficiency, your omission could be a violation of the Civil Rights Act, Title VII unless:

The correct answer is: (B) Speaking fluent English plays a major role in maintaining the safety of the work environment

No employer is allowed to exercise discrimination on the basis of the level of language proficiency an employee or candidate has, unless the candidate or employee's ability to speak English well is fundamental to a safe work environment.

(41)The tendency of the media to choose specific points in a story to promote their definition of the problem highlighted or even interpretation of a causal nature and moral assessment is referred to as:

The correct answer is: (C) Framing

The idea of framing is linked to the tradition of setting an agenda, although it extends its research to focus on the importance of the matters at hand. Going by the framing theory, you will find the media focusing on particular events and then putting them strategically within the scope of the general meaning. Essentially, the media presents information to its audience in a manner to influence the way the audience processes the information. That manner of presentation is the "frame," and it works toward organizing or structuring the meaning of the message. Per this theory, the media not only suggests to the audience what to think of the news it presents, but also how to translate the entire issue.

(42)   There used to be a policy that required media presenters to provide diversified perspectives to controversial issues, to avoid one point of view becoming dominant. However, this policy was repealed in 1987 by the US Congress. That original policy was the:

The correct answer is: (D) Fairness doctrine

This doctrine of fairness was a policy of the Federal Communications Commission (FCC), and the commission's belief at the time was that the licenses issued for broadcasting, be it radio or TV, were essentially a kind of public trust. So the broadcasting stations owed the public balance and fairness while covering contentious issues.

It was the Reagan administration that rendered that policy ineffective. As a result, the FCC was unable to encourage objective debate of controversial issues via the media. It is important to note that this fairness doctrine is entirely different from the Equal Time Rule. Per the 1934 act, broadcasting stations are required to offer an equal amount of time to all candidates running for political office as long as they are considered qualified in the legal sense of the word.

(43)   Some of the biggest _____ based in the United States include Weber Shandwick, Ketchum Inc., FleishmanHillard Inc. and Hill+Knowlton Strategies.

The correct answer is: (C) Public relations agencies

The process of communicating with the media and stakeholders is referred to as public relations (PR).

It is advisable for a firm or individuals in the public limelight to engage the services of a PR agency for the sake of building, protecting and enhancing their reputation using media channels. Good agencies are able to analyze you or your organization with a view to pinpointing positive aspects and sharing these with the media to build your reputation.

(44)   Among the entities listed below, one reports to the US Congress directly and does not consult with the US State Department in its operations. Which is it?

The correct answer is: (D) The Broadcasting Board of Governors

The US Broadcasting Board of Governors (BBG) comprises the US-based civilian international broadcasting corporations that include Voice of America, Radio Free Europe, Radio Liberty, Radio Free Asia and Radio & TV Marti, as well as the Middle East Broadcasting Networks, which are composed of Radio Sawa and Alhurra Television.

Broadcasters under the BBG distribute programming in 61 languages via radio and TV as well as the internet and other media, reaching up to 278 million people. The BBG strives to disseminate information and provide news as well as other worthwhile discussions on a global level, and to be a good example of a professional free press.

(45)   The Smith-Mundt Act, which is basically the United States' Information & Educational Exchange Act of 1948 (IEEA), deters the government from:

The correct answer is: (C) Releasing information meant for foreign audiences to audiences within the United States

The purpose of the IEEA as an initiative for educational exchange is to enhance the world's understanding of the United States and strengthen international relations. Before this act was passed, similar programs were infrequently conducted in the United States, and only with a few select countries. For instance, in 1940 Nelson Rockefeller initiated an exchange program between the United States and Latin America, whereby, as the Commercial & Cultural Affairs for the American Republics coordinator, he invited 130 journalists from the region to come to the United States. After World War II, Karl E. Mundt, the representative for South Dakota, together with New Jersey Senator H. Alexander Smith, introduced a bill that became the IEEA.

(46)   The citizens of the United States are prohibited from listening to or reading certain materials meant for the outreach of public diplomacy owing to some acts passed by Congress. These acts include:

The correct answer is: (D) Smith-Mundt

Fulbright-Hayes is an act passed in 1961 that provides for the enhancement of strong US relations at the international level through the global promotion of mutual acceptance among people by way of educational and cultural exchanges. McCain-Feingold is a 2002 congressional act that came about through bipartisan campaign reform and sought to regulate political campaigns' financing.

(47)   One of the entities or programs listed below is an official American government body involved in public diplomacy initiatives. Which one is it?

The correct answer is: (C) The International Visitors Leadership Program

The International Visitors Leadership Program (IVLP) is a premier exchange program run by the US government. It involves visits to the United States on a short-term basis by current and upcoming leaders of foreign countries whose leadership can be in diverse fields. The aim is not only to enhance the skills those foreigners have by exposing them firsthand to the US experience, but also to create relationships with Americans in their respective fields. Meetings are held in which these professionals showcase the interest they have professionally and discuss areas in which they are able to support US foreign policy.

The number of visitors entering the United States under the IVLP every year is close to 5,000, and over 200,000 have made contact with US citizens via the program over time. Over 500 of those are sitting heads of government, chiefs of state or individuals who have held those positions in the past.

(48)   During the 1960s and 1970s, Tom Wolfe, Joan Didion, Gay Talese and others like them were known to often take their sources' point of view when they wrote. That kind of reporting was referred to as:

The correct answer is: (D) New journalism

New journalism evolved in the 1960s and 1970s. It is dominated by subjective perspectives and its literary style emphasizes the truth as opposed to the facts.

This form of reporting was intensive, and reporters were totally immersed in the stories they were writing. It was a form of journalism that went contrary to traditional methods of journalism that typically keep journalists out of sight or invisible, with plain facts being reported with utmost objectivity. This type of journalism ended by the early 1980s.

(49)   How attractive a culture and its values are can increase a country's importance on the international scene. Which of the terms listed below is often used in reference to such an impact?

The correct answer is: (D) Soft power

The term "soft power" refers to an approach of persuasion used in international relations, ordinarily using cultural or economic influences.

The Marshall Plan is a good example of soft power used by the US government. So are cultural exchanges that the United States uses to make a good impression on foreign countries. The United States also uses the internet as soft power when it consciously portrays a country with great freedom of expression. One expert has described soft power as the capacity to achieve what you target by way of attraction as opposed to coercion. Some countries offer to assist others economically, which is essentially the use of soft power to influence the beneficiary of such assistance.

Soft power is contrary to "hard power," which is more explicit and predictable. Hard power is reflected by the use of the military or other forms of coercion and intimidation. Among the major advantages of soft power is being able to influence other countries without incurring the costs associated with hard power, such as animosity between countries, loss of lives and high expenditures in military equipment.

(50)   Suppose there are editorials in a newspaper called Lapatria condemning the United States' refusal to provide a country with assistance. Which option listed below is best taken by an officer serving in the foreign office?

The correct answer is: (B) Get booklets printed and issue press releases making it known that the United States is interested in enhancing philanthropic initiatives in both the private and public sectors in the country

This way, the foreign officer would be emphasizing the positive attitude of the US government toward donor funding and trying to influence the thinking of local audiences, effectively countering negative press that the United States is deliberately refusing to increase donor funding.

(51) Which of the following US presidents served two non-consecutive terms?

The correct answer is: (A) Grover Cleveland

Grover Cleveland served as the 22nd and 24th president of the United States. He was a lawyer by profession and became president in 1885, with his first term ending in 1889. He was later reelected to office in 1893 and served as president up to 1897. A Democrat, he was elected to office at a time when political leadership in the United States was dominated by the Republican Party.

(52)   The government's reason for creating the Warren Commission was:

The correct answer is: (D) To investigate the assassination of John F. Kennedy

President Lyndon B. Johnson formed the Warren Commission in 1963 to investigate the assassination of President Kennedy. Killed while in office on November 22, 1963, Kennedy was the 35th US president.

(53)   The Scopes Trial revolved around:

The correct answer is: (C) Teaching of evolution in US schools

The Scopes Trial, also referred to as the Scopes Monkey Trial, took place in 1925. It was a legal suit in which a substitute teacher was accused of violating the Tennessee Butler Act that made it illegal to teach the evolution of the human race to US students in schools funded by the state. The teacher's name was John Thomas Scopes.

Although Scopes' conviction required him to pay a fine of $100, he was later pronounced not guilty by the Supreme Court on technical grounds even as it upheld that the statute under which he had been convicted was constitutional.

(54)   Who was the Roman emperor involved in building a huge wall running across the northern part of Britain in AD 122?

The correct answer is (A) Emperor Hadrian

When people refer to Hadrian's Wall, which in Latin is Rigore Valli Aeli, or the line running along the Hadrian frontier, they are talking about a fortification of stone plus turf that the Roman Empire built, stretching across the entire width of today's England.

(55)   Who wrote what is referred to as "the 95 theses"?

The correct answer is: (B) Martin Luther

Martin Luther, a professor of theology of German descent, found the Catholic Church overindulgent and led a revolt against the church, culminating in the formation of Europe's Protestant movement. He was against the church's practice of granting indulgences, whereby a person's sin was expiated after the person paid a certain amount. Sometimes people would buy the certificates for the sake of someone they believed was in purgatory. Luther considered this practice to be preying upon people.

(56)   The US Constitution has _____ amendments so far.

The correct answer is: (D) 27

The US Constitution has 27 amendments so far, and the 27th was proposed for the first time in 1789 and ratified in 1992. The amendment stipulates that any proposed change to congressional members' pay should take effect only after the following election for members of the House.

(57) Choose the option that best describes who Stamford Raffles was.

The correct answer is: (C) Singapore's founder

The full name of Singapore's founder was Sir Thomas Stamford Raffles, and he was British. This statesman, who served as British Java's lieutenant governor from 1811 to 1815 before becoming Bencoolen's governor general from 1817 to 1822, became most prominent for founding Singapore.

(58) _____ fought against the combined forces of Uruguay, Brazil and Argentina from 1864 to 1870?

The correct answer is: (D) Paraguay

The Paraguayan War, also referred to as the "War of the Triple Alliance," was a military conflict within South America with Paraguay on one side and armies from three other countries—Brazil, Uruguay and Argentina—on the other. This conflict raged from 1864 to 1870 and ultimately had international consequences.

Initially the war was between Paraguay and Brazil, but in 1865 the other two countries joined as Brazil's allies and the combined forces ended up defeating Paraguay.

(59) Who founded Afghanistan?

The correct answer is: (A) Ahmad Shah Abdali

Actually, Ahmad Shah Abdali founded the entire Durrani Empire, so he is taken to be the founder of what is known as the Afghanistan state.

(60) The belief that it is good to raise taxes in order to assist the poor exemplifies:

The correct answer is: (C) A normative economic statement

In the fields of economics and philosophy, a value judgment is expressed using a normative statement that shows if a given scenario is desirable or otherwise, but in a subjective manner. It is a way of looking at the current world the way it "ought" to be.

(61) From an economic perspective, the items listed below, apart from one, can be shown in a PPF. Which is that exception?

The correct answer is: (A) Consumer preference

"PPF" stands for "production-possibility frontier." It is also sometimes referred to as "PPC" or production-possibility curve. It graphically depicts different combinations of quantity of goods that can be produced with the available resources and technology. Through the PPF you can see the different outputs possible as products are produced in a combined approach. In this question, the only item in the list of options that is not possible to depict in a PPF is consumer preference.

(62)   The way price mechanism works is mostly through:

The correct answer is: (B) Incentives and signaling

In a market economy, decisions are made based on price mechanism, which is based on two invisible forces, namely demand and supply. Demand refers to the quantity of goods and services that consumers are prepared to buy at a given price within a specified time period.

Incentive is used for something offered to producers or consumers to encourage them to act a certain way. For producers, an increase in price of their commodity serves as motivation for them to supply more of the commodity, as they anticipate more revenue coupled with higher profits.

Whereas producers want to produce and supply more when prices are high and new suppliers want to enter the market, consumers want to reduce the amount they buy or completely stop buying the commodity.

(63)   Where is the Cordillera de los Frailes, located within the cities of Potosi and Oruro, geographically situated?

The correct answer is: (A) Bolivia

The Cordillera de los Frailes is a mountainous region within the central area of the Bolivian Andes.

(64)   There are _____ countries bordering China.

The correct answer is: (D) 14

The countries that directly border China are India, Nepal and Pakistan; Bhutan, Afghanistan and North Korea; Tajikistan, Vietnam and Kazakhstan; Russia, Laos and Myanmar; plus Mongolia and Kyrgyzstan.

(65)   The country with the biggest population on the African continent is:

The correct answer is (A) Nigeria

Nigeria is in the top 10 countries with the highest population in the world. Its population in 2019 was estimated at over 200 million.

(66)   The mountain considered highest in South America when its height is taken right from sea level up to the top is:

The correct answer is: (C) Aconcagua

Aconcagua is 6,960.8 m or 22,837 feet high and is the highest peak in the Western and Southern Hemispheres.

(67)   There is a capital city in Latin America that was developed in the region where Tenochtitlan, the capital of the Aztec Empire, existed. Which is that city?

The correct answer is: (B) Mexico City

Mexico City was built where the city of Tenochtitlan once existed. That ancient city, Tenochtitlan, thrived from AD 1325 to AD 1521. It was built on an island on Lake Texcoco, with a canal system and causeways facilitating the delivery of supplies to the thousands of people who lived there.

(68)   It is more appropriate to maintain a focus on intangible rewards and corporate culture as opposed to adherence to stringent rules when:

The correct answer is: (A) The work involved entails creativity and self-direction

When the work being done requires the individuals involved to be highly creative and independent, it is best to focus on the corporate culture and intangible rewards because of the particular motivations of these types of employees.

(69)   It would be beneficial to use performance management as a substitute for:

The correct answer is: (C) Traditional appraisal systems

One can successfully use performance management as a substitute for the traditional method of employee appraisal. This type of review entails looking at an employee's full scope of work performance from the day he or she is hired.

(70)   In order to reduce the incidence of work-related stress among employees in an organization, management can employ an easy, cost-effective strategy that entails:

The correct answer is: (D) Planning ahead to minimize or entirely eliminate crises

Often employees get stressed because they are so often in crisis-management mode. Whatever the work involved, if there is almost always a crisis to be managed, it can make it very stressful for everyone involved. As such, option (D) is the best because it keeps crises to a minimum.

Having an open layout is not the solution, as it is sometimes uncomfortably noisy and can make it difficult to complete tasks because of the many distractions. Giving only minimal responsibilities is not helpful with regard to stress reduction, as it can end up making the employees insecure about the jobs they hold. Extreme competition among employees can actually be a cause of stress in itself.

(71) The Missouri Compromise:

The correct answer is: (B) Accepted Maine as a free state in the Union and Missouri as a slave state

The Missouri Compromise was the US Congress' effort to defuse the rivalries that existed between sections of the community and people with varying political ideologies, which had been triggered by a request made by Missouri to have the state admitted into the Union even as slavery continued. This request was made in 1819. This was a time when the United States had just 22 states, with those for slavery and against it being equal in number.

(72) How many members within the US House of Representatives are qualified to vote?

The correct answer is: (B) 435

There are 435 members comprising the US House of Representatives.

The US government has two legislative bodies, one being the Senate and the other the House of Representatives. While each member of the Senate represents a whole state, each member of the House of Representatives represents a district within a state. This means one state can have more than one House representative, depending on how populous the state is. One term for a House representative lasts two years, while one term for a senator lasts six years.

In total, the number of voting House members are 435, and six members have no voting rights. The latter is composed of representatives of Puerto Rico, the District of Columbia and American Samoa, as well as the Northern Mariana Islands, Guam and the Virgin Islands.

(73) The US political party that started the system of using national conventions in the nomination process of presidential candidates was:

The correct answer is: (D) The Anti-Masonic Party

The US political scene saw the entry of a third party when strong opposition to Freemasonry led to the formation of the Anti-Masonic Party. The first two dominant political parties in the country were the Federalist Party and the Republican Party. Later on, the Anti-Masonic Party began to embrace other issues in a bid to have its members elected, and it became the first party to rely on national conventions for nomination of its presidential candidate.

(74) One conqueror who became famous in the fifth century was referred to as "The Scourge of God." What was his real name?

The correct answer is: (A) Attila the Hun

Attila the Hun ruled the Huns from AD 434 to 453. He was the enemy who caused fear through the western and eastern areas of the Roman Empire, and that won him admirers who gave him the name "Scourge of God." He captivated them with the success of his attacks and his prowess in destroying great cities, such as Constantinople.

(75)Which of the people listed below did not live in the sixth century BC?

The correct answer is: (C) Nero

Emperor Nero became emperor of the Roman Empire in AD 37 following the death of Emperor Claudius, Nero's adopted father. Nero was mostly known for his cruelty and depravity. He committed suicide in AD 68, ending the dynasty that historians refer to as the "Julio-Claudius" dynasty.

(76) The _____ Empire ended after the Goth invasion that took place during the fifth century.

The correct answer is: (A) Roman

The Goths are the people who sacked Rome in AD 410. They were people of East German origin, and two of their branches, the Visigoths and Ostrogoths, contributed in a major way to the disintegration of the Western Roman Empire. They did this by waging a long-running series of wars, referred to as the Gothic Wars. As the empire came to an end, Medieval Europe emerged.

(77)In 1991, the _____ revolution caused Soviet troops to withdraw from Czechoslovakia.

The correct answer is: (C) Velvet

The Velvet Revolution refers to the peaceful transition the state of Czechoslovakia underwent as it ceased to be communist. The revolution itself, which is sometimes referred to as the Gentle Revolution, took place in December 1989, and it was nonviolent. It led to the departure of Soviet troops from Czechoslovakia in 1991 after a successful democratic election had taken place in June 1990, the first of its nature since 1946.

(78)   The leader famously known for crossing the Rubicon is:

The correct answer is: (D) Julius Caesar

Julius Caesar decided to defy the Roman senate and cross the Rubicon in 49 BC, and his action led to civil war as he fought to expand the Roman Republic into the Roman Empire. Among his conquests was the triumph against the Gauls, who lived in what is today known as France, a campaign that ended in 51 BC with the execution of Vercingetorix, who led the Gauls in the fight. Today, "to cross the Rubicon" is a phrase used for an action that is irrevocable; meaning, the person who takes the action has reached a point where there is no choice but to pursue a certain cause.

(79)   China's capital in 1928 was:

The correct answer is: (B) Nanjing

Nanjing actually means "South Capital." Nanjing became China's capital during the Ming Dynasty in 1368, and also in 1927 when the Nationalist Party led by Chiang Kai-shek declared it the country's capital.

(80)   If a government intervenes in a bid to correct an apparent failure within the market, this is said to be inefficient if:

The correct answer is: (C) The overall cost of implementing the action proves greater than the resulting benefit

What one needs to do is calculate the benefit-cost ratio (BCR), and the result can then be used in summarizing the general value for the amount of money set aside or proposed for a given project. In fact, BCR is just a ratio of the overall benefits expected from a project or proposal, expressed in terms of money against the anticipated costs.

(81) If you have a good known as X and another known as Y, and if X's price rises in tandem with Y's demand, X and Y are said to be:

The correct answer is: (D) Substitutes

When the demand of a given good rises following the rise in the price of another good, it basically means the two goods serve the same purpose; this is the reason one can be substituted for the other by the consumer. It means the consumer does not need to contend with the increased price of either of the two items.

By the same token, a drop of the price of one of those two goods is bound to cause a drop in the demand for the other, even when the good with reduced demand has its price unaltered. The reason is that many consumers will opt to purchase the good whose price has dropped.

(82) If you have a good known as X and another known as Y, and if X's price rises as Y's demand drops, X and Y are said to be:

The correct answer is: (B) Complements

If a good contributes something that makes the other better or more appealing to consumers, the two goods can be termed complementary. In short, if consumers find it not worthwhile to buy a particular good because they cannot afford to buy another specific one, those two goods can be correctly referred to as complementary goods.

For example, consumers would not have any use for ink if pens were not affordable, and demand for ink cartridges would drop if the price of printers rose too high for potential buyers to afford them.

(83) To the west of the Continental Divide is the state capital of:

The correct answer is: (A) Salem

Salem is a city within a valley in the state of Oregon, and the Willamette River runs right through it. There are other places in the United States called Salem, but they are not along the Continental Divide. Montgomery is the capital city of Alabama, also in the United States, but it is close to the Gulf of Mexico, while Colombia is in the northwestern part of South America, with some of its parts within North America. As for Frankfort, it is the capital city of Kentucky.

(84)   The country sometimes referred to as the "Teardrop of India" and which was officially known as Ceylon in the past is:

The correct answer is: (D) Sri Lanka

Sri Lanka is a tiny island situated right within the south of the Indian peninsula, and it is shaped like a teardrop. Formerly it was known as Ceylon, a name given to it by the British when it was a colony. Although it gained independence from Britain in 1948, the island fully became a republic in 1972, and that was when it changed its name to Sri Lanka.

(85)   The tiniest independent country in the whole world with regard to its geographical area is:

The correct answer is: (C) The Vatican

The Vatican is the tiniest country in the world, measuring a paltry 44 hectares, or 110 acres. The country is also known as the Holy See and is headed by the pope. The Vatican, which is the Catholic Church's center or headquarters, is within Rome, which is itself the capital of Italy.

(86)   The mountain considered the highest in the entire world when its measurement is taken right from the level of its own oceanic base is:

The correct answer is: (B) Mauna Kea

Mauna Kea is a dormant volcano in Hawaii and stands at 4,205 meters above sea level. In fact, the biggest part of this mountain is below sea level, extending beyond 10,000 meters downwards. When measured right from the ocean base of Mauna Kea, the mountain even beats Mt. Everest in height.

(87)   Among the actions listed below, one does not always enhance competition among companies. Which one is it?

The correct answer is: (D) Industry deregulation

Deregulation of any industry is not necessarily tantamount to increased competition among existing companies. Whether competition will increase or decrease is mainly dependent on the particular regulations that have been removed.

As for there being several competitors and slow industry growth, these both lead to companies trying to lure clients from one another to maintain their growth. High overhead costs make existing companies work extra hard to remain competitive, and it is mainly the companies aspiring to enter the industry that are discouraged.

(88)   To avoid high staff turnover when the industry is very competitive, a company should:

The correct answer is: (C) Introduce programs geared toward employee retention

It is advisable for a company to introduce programs geared toward employee retention in a competitive industry, as high employee turnover causes difficulties in implementing bigger strategies. When skilled employees leave in the middle of a project, the company has to strive to fill the gap, and the teams might take a long time to work together again cohesively.

Among the factors that can be considered in an employee retention program are improved health and retirement benefits, perks within the workplace and chances to take up company stock options.

(89)   One of the options below did not contribute to the prosperity of America during the 1950s.

The correct answer is: (D) Introduction of computer technology

Although the computer was invented during the 1950s, computer technology did not influence the prospering of America at that time. During that period, only a few big companies used computers, and computer technology did not become a significant force in the country's development until some decades later.

(90)   Which of the options listed below contributed to people's rapid shift to the suburbs?

The correct answer is: (A) Hope of bigger, safer homes

The prospects of occupying houses that were not only bigger but also safer than those within urban centers lured many people to the suburbs. In America, loans were offered to stimulate development of housing in the suburbs, and many people chose to move to those areas because the lots on which individual houses were built were larger. Still, growth of suburbs did not deter cities from growing.

(91) With regards to children, Dr. Spock told women to:

The correct answer is: (B) Be affectionate with their children and trust their personal instincts

Dr. Benjamin McLane Spock was an American pediatrician who wrote a best-selling book on the care of babies and children. He assured mothers that they know more about the welfare of their children than they sometimes believe they do. He asked mothers to take their instincts seriously when it came to raising their children. Dr. Spock's teachings were contradictory to earlier teachings that focused a lot on disciplining children.

(92)   During the Space Race, the United States managed to _____ before the USSR.

The correct answer is: (C) Put a man on the moon

Neil Armstrong and Buzz Aldrin became the first men to land on the moon when the United States used spaceflight Apollo II from July 16, 1969, to July 24, 1969. Although Russia managed to send an earlier unmanned vessel into space, they have not yet managed to send a man to the moon. According to a July 2019 report in the UK's Telegraph, Russia now hopes to accomplish the feat by 2030.

(93)   Rock 'n' roll and the Beat Generation had something in common. What was it?

The correct answer is: (A) Resistance to conformity during the 1950s

The Beat Generation was begun by some authors as a literary movement, and through their work they endeavored to explore and influence American culture and politics. This was the era immediately following the major world wars.

As for rock 'n' roll, it is a music genre whose origin evolved in the late 1940s and early 1950s. This music has its roots in gospel, country music, rhythm & blues, jazz and jump blues, as well as boogie-woogie.

(94)　During his final formal address, President Eisenhower warned the people of America against:

The correct answer is: (C) The military industrial complex

During his final address as US president, Eisenhower alerted Americans that there could be a danger posed by the military industrial complex. He felt that Americans did not quite understand how strong the influence on government could be from the individuals and organizations engaged in production of military technology and weapons in general. This network of participants endeavors to gain political support so that the government increases its spending on military equipment.

(95)　President Kennedy's legislative efforts were continually blocked by the:

The correct answer is: (A) Southern Democrats

The Southern Democrats were a conservative group who eventually left the Democratic Party to join the Republican Party.

(96)　The primary group involved in sit-ins, which entailed protesting against segregation within the Southern states, was composed of

The correct answer is: (D) Students of black descent

Students of black descent were mainly responsible for the sit-ins that protested segregation in America's Southern states. The sit-ins were peaceful and involved students sitting at specific lunch counters and refusing to leave until they had been served.

(97)   The sheriff who terrified Americans with his violent acts and whose brutality ended up winning sympathy for the ongoing civil rights movement was:

The correct answer is: (B) Eugene "Bull" Connor

Bull Connor was the sheriff of Alabama who terrified Americans. His brutal acts included using dogs to terrify children and small tanks to assault protestors. His tactics became a symbol of racism in the Southern states.

(98)   The Cuban Missile Crisis resulted in _____, among other things.

The correct answer is: (D) The Nuclear Test Ban Treaty being signed

The Cuban Missile Crisis is also referred to as the October Crisis of 1962, and sometimes it is referred to as the Caribbean Crisis or the Missile Scare. It was a confrontation that took place between the United States and the Soviet Union back and started when America discovered the Soviet Union had deployed ballistic missiles to Cuba. Khrushchev and Cuban President Fidel Castro had secretly agreed that the Soviet Union would place ballistic missiles in Cuba and build facilities to help launch the missiles, all in the effort to protect Cuba from any attacks from the United States.

During the standoff between the two world powers, they both realized how easy it was to begin a nuclear war that was dangerous to everyone involved. Therefore, at the end of the Cold War they decided to sign a treaty banning the testing or use of nuclear missiles.

(99)   According to President Johnson, _____ gave him leeway to escalate the Vietnam conflict.

The correct answer is: (A) The Gulf of Tonkin Resolution

Since the Gulf of Tonkin Resolution permitted President Johnson to render assistance to any country that threatened aggression, he translated that to mean that it also accorded him the right as US president to escalate the Vietnam conflict.

(100) In the United States, The Weathermen were:

The correct answer is: (B) A violent student organization with political inclinations in the 1960s and 1970s

This organization known as The Weathermen was violent, with some activities including bombing banks and the U.S. capitol. The group bombed the Pentagon and the State Department. Nevertheless, they made sure they warned the people in those places to evacuate before they carried out the bombings.

(101) The issue that most significantly united the New Left during the late 1960s was:

The correct answer is: (B) Opposition to the war in Vietnam

All the issues listed in the answer options were important to some people in the New Left, but the issue that people in that category unanimously opposed was the continuing war in Vietnam. The Vietnam War began when the United States began sending military advisors and other assistance to the government of South Vietnam in a bid to counter the influence of China's communist ideologies.

(102) The "termination" approach to Native Americans by the US government argued for:

The correct answer is: (C) Elimination of recognition of Native American tribes as legal entities

If the termination approach had succeeded, it would have meant the end of Native American tribes being recognized as legal entities. In present-day America, these tribes still retain some sovereignty within the reservations, albeit limited, and they are not subject to the laws of their states.

(103) The Marielitos were:

The correct answer is: (A) People of Cuban origin who came to the United States in 1980

The people of Cuban origin who are referred to as Marielitos immigrated to America in 1980, using boats from Mariel Harbor. These boatlifts took place from April 1980 up to October the same year, and they ceased when the United States and Cuba mutually agreed to halt the boatlifts. By the time these boatlifts stopped, they had transported 125,000 Cubans to America.

One of the reasons so many Cubans tried to leave Cuba at the time was that the Cuban economy was doing badly, although there were a good number of Cubans who were also trying to leave for political reasons.

(104) Cesar Chavez is remembered for:

The correct answer is: (B) Organizing Hispanic workers in the agricultural sector

The main reason Cesar Chavez continues to be remembered in US history is that he organized Hispanic agricultural workers and, together with Dolores Huerta, established the National Farm Workers Association. This organization later became United Farm Workers.

(105) The very first woman in America to be on the ticket of one of the dominant political parties during a presidential election was:

The correct answer is: (D) Geraldine Ferrero

Geraldine Ferrero was selected by Walter Mondale, who was a presidential candidate during 1984, to be his running mate. That Democratic Party ticket did not win, but Ferrero made history not only as the sole Italian American to have vied at a national level for a major party, but for becoming the first woman in the United States to have sought such a high political office for a major party.

In that election, Mondale, who had served as vice president to Jimmy Carter, lost to Ronald Reagan, who had George H. W. Bush as his running mate on a Republican Party ticket.

(106) The constitutional justification for the ruling of the Roe v. Wade case was:

The correct answer is: (A) Right to privacy

Protecting the constitutional right to privacy was the justification for the ruling of Roe v. Wade. Consequently, abortion was legalized. According to the Supreme Court, a person's right to privacy is implied, though is not explicitly detailed in the Constitution.

It was the Supreme Court's view that this particular right was fundamental in fulfilling some other rights already listed in the Constitution.

(107) The reason Nixon could venture into China was:

The correct answer is: (D) He was known to be zealously against communism

Relations between China and the United States had been bad for a whole 25 years before President Nixon paid China a visit in 1972. In 1973 efforts began to formally establish a US liaison office in Beijing. Americans could see that Nixon's actions merely constituted a realpolitik move, considering how much Nixon was against communism.

If any other American, politician or otherwise, had tried to do what President Nixon did, accusations would have been leveled against them for harboring secret sympathy for the communists. Formal diplomatic relations between the United States and China were not established until 1979.

(108) The reason for the plummeting of President's Ford's popularity was:

The correct answer is: (C) His decision to pardon Richard Nixon

Although President Ford became less popular after pardoning Nixon, he did so in a bid to save the United States from the constant distraction of the crimes Nixon was said to have committed. Ford thought that dealing with the crimes Nixon had been accused of, which was bound to take place in the public arena, was not good for the country, and that letting him off the hook would make Americans move quickly onto other issues of more national importance.

(109) By the time President Jimmy Carter's term in office came to an end, the U.S. economy _____.

The correct answer is: (D) Had record-high interest and inflation rates

By the time President Carter left office in 1981, inflation in the United States was high and the economy appeared stagnant. Nevertheless, these problems had been there when he took over office, although the recession that began in 1973 was resolved by 1975.

Jimmy Carter actually created over nine million jobs, although the Iranian hostage crisis marred his presidency and the rising inflation did not help his popularity.

(110)   Ronald Reagan was the most popular candidate in 1984's presidential race. He won in all the US states, apart from:

The correct answer is: (A) Minnesota

Ronald Reagan, whose major rival in the 1984 presidential elections was Walter Mondale, ended up winning every single state in America apart from Mondale's home state—Minnesota. Nevertheless, even in this one state, Mondale's win was not very impressive, beating Reagan by just a fifth of a single percent.

(111)   Supply-side economics is based on the theory that:

The correct answer is: (B) Reducing taxes will succeed in spurring the economy

The thinking is that once people enjoy tax cuts, they will be motivated to invest more, and then those investments will have the effect of spurring the growth of the economy. Thus, everyone will benefit—both investors and consumers.

(112)   One achievement attributed to President Bill Clinton is:

The correct answer is: (D) Balancing the US federal budget

President Bill Clinton managed to balance the US federal budget in his second term in office. Despite the bitter rivalry that existed between the president and the Republican Party, he succeeded in gaining support across the board and got important legislation passed.

(113)   All options listed below except one accurately explain changes in the American economy during the late 1980s and 1990s. Which option does not explain the changes?

The correct answer is: (B) For the first time in a century, America experienced its lowest rate of poverty

The United States did not actually experience the lowest rate of poverty in a century. In fact, it was during the 1980s and 1990s that most US families found it necessary to take up additional jobs in order to supplement their major source of income and manage to maintain their usual standard of living.

(114)   At the end of the 20th century, some major achievements in the field of technology occurred. Which of the choices listed below does not constitute one of those achievements?

The correct answer is: (A) Development in Texas of the Superconducting Super Collider

The Superconducting Super Collider project was never finished. It was envisioned as the greatest particle accelerator in the world, but after a decade's work the cost that had originally been projected to total $4 billion exceeded that figure and reached a whopping $12 billion. Thus the project was canceled.

(115)   The strong US political movement that supports candidates who are anti-abortion is:

The correct answer is: (C) The right-to-life movement

The right-to-life movement votes only for those candidates who specifically promise that they will oppose women's right to abortion. The other answers include groups that disagree with abortion, but the right-to-life movement's central focus is anti-abortion.

(116)   Which of the options listed below does not have a record of being opposed to globalization?

The correct answer is: (B) The International Monetary Fund

The International Monetary Fund (IMF) is not on record as ever opposing the idea of globalization. In fact, the first time there was great opposition to the idea of globalization was during the Seattle incident when protestors from groups that ordinarily pursue disparate agendas converged to protest the World Trade Organization meeting in 1999.

(117)   The longest war in US history was:

The correct answer is: (C) The Vietnam War

The Vietnam War lasted the longest, not the war in Afghanistan, which is frequently a mistake made by the media. The reason the media is wrong in finding the Vietnam War shorter is that they consider 1964 to be the beginning of the war, but before the Gulf of Tonkin Resolution, there had already been US soldiers fighting inside Vietnam since 1961.

(118)   The period when the United States experienced the highest level of unemployment was:

The correct answer is: (A) The Great Depression

The Great Depression was when unemployment in the United States was at its highest, and it has never been so high again. In 1932, the unemployment level in the United States hit a depressing 23.6%.

(119)   With the knowledge you have of the region's geography, which of the choices below would you say was a key activity that was economically affected by Israel's victory in 1967's Six-Day War?

The correct answer is: (D) Transportation of products via the Suez Canal

The economic activity most impacted by the Six-Day War was the transportation of goods using the Suez Canal.

(120)   Which option below best explains the difference in urbanization between Germany and Portugal?

The correct answer is: (D) Germany happens to be in the middle of Europe's industrial belt

Germany is right in the center of Europe's industrial belt, but Portugal is not within that region. Other countries that are part of the industrial belt of Europe include France and Italy, as well as Great Britain.

(121) _____ imports most of the wheat consumed in the country.

The correct answer is: (C) Japan

Japan imports a lot of wheat from the United States and Canada as well as Australia, which makes up around 90% of the wheat it consumes. However, this position may soon change when the free trade agreement reached between the EU and Japan in 2018 takes effect. The possible success of the Comprehensive and Progressive Agreement for Trans-Pacific Partnership that replaced the Trans-Pacific Partnership that included the United States is also likely to affect the amount of wheat Japan continues to import from the United States.

(122) Which of the methods listed below is most accurately depicts the level of desertification within a given region?

The correct answer is: (C) Satellite imagery

Satellite imagery provides highly accurate visual evidence when it comes to determining how extensive a region's desertification is.

(123) Of the countries listed below, _____ is the one with the greatest trade with the United States in regards to volume and value.

The correct answer is: (C) Canada

Among all the countries the United States trades with, Canada is the largest single trade partner in terms of volume and value of goods.

(124) In America, the Midwest's fertile soil is a result of:

The correct answer is: (A) Glaciers

A glacier forms after mountain snow or snow around the North or South Pole accumulates and becomes compact. As glacier moves, it usually deposits massive mounds of soil and mud, and even gravel, tiny rocks and sand.

All these deposits are referred to as "till," and it is created when the rocks and soil beneath the glaciers get ground up to form "moraines" on a glacier's surface and sides.

(125)   Which of the statements listed below is true of developing countries' economies?

The correct answer is: (A) The goods they export are mainly raw agricultural materials

It is true that most goods from developing countries are predominantly raw agricultural products. As a result, developing countries end up importing the products processed from their raw materials at much higher prices, making the developed countries the net beneficiaries. In addition to the exports from developing countries being raw, they are also limited in number, with some countries exporting just one or two items.

(126)   Women are more adversely affected by desertification in East African countries than men because:

The correct answer is: (B) Women are the ones mainly in charge of gathering wood for fuel and water for domestic use

Women in East African countries have for a long time been responsible for collecting water for domestic use. In areas that are arid or semi-arid, women walk long distances to find water, which in many cases is not clean enough to be recommended for drinking, yet such a find is considered precious. In the meantime, the men travel far away from home to earn a monetary income or stay home and farm the land.

(127)   The forces of gravity, wind, ice and water have an effect on the general natural environment because:

The correct answer is: (A) They highly contribute to erosion

When there is erosion, lands that are normally great for agriculture are left with poor soils that cannot sustain enough crops and animals, while hills and mountains that used to hold trees, shrubs and other vegetation become poorer in terms of the quality and number of plants they have. Consequently, natural animal habitats are destroyed and the ecosystem is inevitably altered.

(128) There are times when El Niño, the warm ocean current, is replaced by the cooler Peru current. This happens along the Peruvian coastline, and as a result, anchovies that seabirds rely on for food decrease. Owing to that shortage of birds, there is a drop in the number of birds left to roost along the Peruvian coastal islands. In the country of Peru, such developments negatively affect the:

The correct answer is: (D) Quantities of anchovies exported

Anchovies are tiny forage fish that belong to the Engraulidae family. Most of their species are found within marine water, although there are others that exist in brackish water. There are also some anchovies in South America that are confined to fresh waters.

(129) One set of countries in a zone with a tropical climate is:

The correct answer is: (C) Uganda, Indonesia and Panama

Tropical climates ordinarily have weather that is hot and humid, and a lot of the regions that make up the world's equatorial belt experience this climate. Places with a tropical climate enjoy an abundance of rainfall, and some have frequent thunderstorms.

(130) _____ in Canada is inaccessible using any of the main highways.

The correct answer is: (A) The area of Northwest Territories

Canada's Northwest Territories contain Dehcho and North Slave, South Slave and Sahtu and Inuvik. The landscape is remote and has forests and mountains as well as arctic tundra and those islands within the Canadian Archipelago in the Arctic.

(131) The physical feature separating Siberia from European Russia is:

The correct answer is: (A) The Ural Mountains

The Ural Mountains are sometimes referred as just "the Urals." They extend roughly from the north and the south via the western part of Russia. This range also extends from the Arctic Ocean coast up to the Ural River, and to the northwestern part of

Kazakhstan. This mountain range constitutes part of the accepted boundary separating Europe from Asia.

(132) The reason that a good number of people living in the Caribbean have West African roots is that:

The correct answer is: (B) West Africans were taken as slaves to work on agricultural plantations

West African people were kidnapped by the British to serve as slaves in the Caribbean colonies. Once in the British colonies, these Africans were made to work on plantations. It is said that as many as 3.1 million people from Africa were shipped as slaves by the British to their colonies between 1662 and 1807.

(133) During the last half century, _____ have/has affected the growth of US suburbs.

The correct answer is: (A) Automobiles

The invention of automobiles made traveling easy and convenient, so people did not have to contend with high housing costs in cities and modern urban centers. Houses in the suburbs are normally cheaper, and people are able to travel to and from urban centers with ease to spend their nonworking hours in the suburbs.

Even before automobiles helped to enhance the development of US suburbs, they first catalyzed the growth of the motel industry because people would travel long distances, knowing they could have stopovers in motels before reaching their various destinations.

(134) The formation of fossil fuels like coal or oil is due to:

The correct answer is: (A) Processes of a geological nature that transform organic matter into compost

Fossil fuel generally refers to fuel from geological material that is organic in nature, which is found buried in the form of combustible deposits after forming from the rotten remnants of animals and plants. Due to pressure from the crust of the earth and exposure to heat for lengthy periods running into millions of calendar years, these fuels turn into natural gas, coal, heavy oils or just crude oil.

(135) The best way to explain diffusion is to note that crops once farmed mainly in the Americas now:

The correct answer is: (A) Are grown in all regions of the world

Once something spreads widely the way ideas do over time, this process is referred to as diffusion.

(136) To the south of latitude 60°, one can generally find:

The correct answer is: (A) Floating icebergs

Icebergs are big pieces of ice formed by fresh water after it has broken off from a glacier or ice shelf. Icebergs float freely in the open water that is normally salty. Icebergs sometimes appear whitish and other times bluish when floating in the salty waters of the sea.

(137) In general, most people today emigrate from their home countries:

The correct answer is: (A) In search of better economic opportunities

Emigration is defined as people's relocation to different countries where they end up residing. Although today most people emigrating do so in search of better economic opportunities, emigrants end up contributing to the growth of the economies of those countries where they take up residence.

(138) When a megalopolis develops, it exemplifies:

(A) Urbanization

The term "megalopolis" is used for a city that is not only massive in size but also greatly populated. It is bigger and more populated than a metropolis, which is also a big, busy city. Sometimes a megalopolis can comprise a number of towns considered one group that forms a huge urban complex. A good example of a megalopolis is the city of New York, when it is considered together with Long Island and other areas around it.

(139) The reason the world's major oil-producing countries joined to form OPEC was that:

The correct answer is: (A) They wanted to have greater control of the oil market and prices

The Organization of Petroleum Exporting Countries (OPEC) was founded by five members in 1960, and now the organization has 15 member nations.

The original members of OPEC, whose headquarters is in Austria's capital, Vienna, were Iran, Iraq, Kuwait, Venezuela and Saudi Arabia. The others that have joined the organization to date include Libya, UAE, Nigeria, Ecuador, Qatar, Angola, Gabon, Algeria, Congo and Equatorial Guinea.

(140) The religion followed by most people in India is:

The correct answer is: (D) Hinduism

The largest religion in India is Hinduism. In fact, 80% of the entire Indian population identifies as Hindu, which means there are almost a billion Hindus in India. In comparison, only slightly over 14% of India's population identifies as Muslim, while the rest, about 6%, follow different religions like Christianity, Sikhism or Buddhism.

(141) The term "Corn Belt" is used for a region whose basis of definition is its:

The correct answer is: (B) Major economic activity

The region referred to as the Corn Belt is an area in the US Midwest that has been predominantly growing corn since the 1850s. Nevertheless, in nonspecific terms, it is used to refer to the entire agricultural region in the Midwest.

(142) Rising population has adversely affected coral reefs in some parts of the world, and one place that faces the greatest threat is:

The correct answer is: (C) Southeast Asia, close to Indonesia and the Philippines

A coral reef is a ridge that forms and grows from coral deposits. Coral itself is the tough, stony substance that forms the reefs.

Ordinarily, coral reefs serve as a natural barrier that protects the shoreline and the communities living close by so they are not adversely affected by dangers such as storms, massive waves and erosion.

(143) Japan is most likely to import its forest products from:

The correct answer is: (A) The United States

Japan imports three million tons of pulp that constitute a third of its annual pulp consumption.

(144) The least populated US region is:

The correct answer is: (C) The Rocky Mountains

The Rocky Mountains are a range of mountains that stretch for 4,800 km and are commonly referred to as "the Rockies." The range covers two countries, beginning in British Columbia, Canada, and extending to New Mexico in the United States.

It was estimated some years ago that the population density in this region was four people for every square kilometer, and some cities in the region have a population exceeding 50,000 people. However, populations in some parts of the mountain range are increasing exponentially, with a place like Jackson Hole, Wyoming, seeing a population rise over a period of 40 years from slightly more than 1,200 to close to 4,500 people.

(145) A city's central area is likely to have:

The correct answer is: (C) Office high-rises

Besides office high-rises, a central business district is likely to have well-established financial institutions, being a place customers find easy to access and security is greater than in other areas of the city.

(146) Which option below is most likely to be found where land is level?

The correct answer is: (D) A railroad, an airport and a city

Many railroads and airports are built on land that is level, and that applies to cities. Particular spots may not necessarily be smooth all throughout, but the general landscape, even when on high ground, is generally level.

(147)   The reason the city of New York has residents from different parts of the world and public-school students speak a wide range of languages is that:

The correct answer is: (C) New York is a port through which people access the United States from elsewhere in the world

New York City, which is situated at one of the world's largest harbors, is the point of entry for many people entering the United States legally. While its population is about 8.5 million, slightly more than three million of these constitute people born out of the country. Meanwhile, the languages spoken in New York can reach a count of 800, making the city exceedingly diverse in linguistic terms.

(148)   Before railroads were built in the United States, _____ were most commonly used to transport commercial items like timber and coal during the mid-19th century.

The correct answer is: (A) Canals and rivers

One reason water transport, particularly through rivers, canals, lakes and oceans, was very popular at one point in time was that its cost was affordable in regards to the transportation of commercial goods.

This mode of transportation influenced the development of big settlements close to navigable waters. Goods would be transported for export from the interior via inland waterways, and those from outside regions would reach the ports at the coast for transportation throughout the country.

(149)   What do areas like the central United States and Argentina's Pampas, as well as countries like Ukraine, Canada and the south central area of Australia, have in common that makes them ideal for wheat production?

The correct answer is: (C) They are all plains

It is important to note that although wheat does well in the areas mentioned, these are not necessarily homogeneous. Different wheat varieties require varying amounts of rainfall; temperatures that vary, both day and night; varying soil conditions; and different farming practices.

(150)   Sometimes you can locate snowy areas within an equatorial region when:

The correct answer is: (C) The area is at a high elevation

Snow formation requires that the temperature within the atmosphere be at freezing point or below. This means temperatures at 0°C or below, which is equivalent to 32°F or below, in addition to there being sufficient moisture within the air.

(151)   The equator runs across which set of countries listed below?

The correct answer is: (D) Ecuador, Kenya and Gabon

The equator also crosses Colombia, Brazil, Uganda, Somalia, Congo, the Democratic Republic of Congo, Indonesia, Sao Tome, Kiribati and the Maldives, making 13 countries in total.

(152)   Traveling by road to Rome from Paris, one passes a major physical barrier. That is:

The correct answer is: (B) The Alps

The Alps is the name of a mountain range that spreads across Europe for an entire 1,200 km. It touches eight countries, namely France, Italy, Switzerland, Slovenia, Austria, Monaco, Germany and Liechtenstein.

(153)   Which of the states listed below shares a similar climate with Alice Springs in Australia?

The correct answer is: (D) Arizona

Arizona is one of the biggest US states and it lies within the southwestern side of the country. The areas of the state that are relatively low in altitude are mainly desert with mild winters and very hot summers. Overall, rainfall in the state of Arizona is little, with most of the state remaining mainly dry.

As for Alice Springs, it is a very remote town found in the northern part of Australia, situated between the cities of Darwin and Adelaide.

(154)   In Ireland, land is mainly used for:

The correct answer is: (A) Mixed farming–growing crops and rearing animals

Ireland has fertile soil and a temperate climate, and the rainfall there is in abundance. In fact, over 740,000 acres of Ireland's arable land is used for crop production, with barley, wheat, oats and other cereals leading other crops in output. As for output from animals, beef and milk are in the lead, constituting about 60% of all of Ireland's agricultural products.

(155)   The pair of natural features that form a big part of Chile's border are:

The correct answer is: (B) The Andes Mountains and the Pacific Ocean

The Andes Mountains, which border Chile, are also referred to as the Andean Mountains, and they are the longest of all the world's mountain ranges. As for the Pacific Ocean, it is another feature marking one side of Chile's border.

(156)   Japan enjoys the best balance of trade with:

The correct answer is: (C) The United States

Japan enjoys the best balance of trade with the United States because overall, the net benefit is for Japan. For instance, in 2018, Japan's imports from the United States, both in the form of goods and services, totaled around $121 billion, whereas US imports from Japan totaled around $179 billion, with automobiles and their spare parts constituting a big chunk of this revenue.

(157) In the United States, the major natural vegetation in areas that now produce corn used to be:

The correct answer is: (A) Forests of broadleaf trees and grasslands

Before people occupied the present-day Corn Belt and began farming it for commercial purposes, the area was mainly covered with oak and hickory forests, with some areas of tall-grass prairies.

(158) There is usually conflict between consumers' preference for manufactured products and energy and:

The correct answer is: (B) Clean environment

The reason for this conflict is that when manufacturing takes place, there are normally pollutants emitted into the environment, some in gaseous form and others as solids. However, for people to feel their living standards are improving, they prefer to make use of manufactured goods. People who mainly consume raw products are considered "third-world" as opposed to advancing to a more developed economy, which entails processing of raw products and manufacturing new products.

(159) It is true to say that in the American Southwest:

The correct answer is: (B) Dry conditions cause water to become a fundamental issue for the public

Some areas in the American Southwest have more cacti than grass, which is a mark of desert-like conditions. Water has for a long time been an issue in this region, and in a bid to encourage people to use water sparingly, at one time in the 1970s Tucson's water department raised water rates significantly.

(160) Trade barriers among _____ were lifted by NAFTA.

The correct answer is: (D) The U.S., Canada and Mexico

NAFTA stands for the North American Free Trade Agreement. It lifted trade barriers between the United States and its neighbors, Canada and Mexico. NAFTA, which took effect in 1994, marked the first time developed countries entered into an economic agreement with a developing country, in this case, Mexico. The effect was to encourage trade among those three countries before engaging in trade with other countries.

(161)   In order to be able to predict the area with the most likelihood of acid rain falling, a scientist would very likely study:

The correct answer is: (C) Wind patterns that normally prevail over areas where significant manufacturing takes place

Rainfall usually becomes acidic when the atmosphere gets extremely polluted, and such rain ends up harming forests and waters. Well-known pollutants include coal, different fossil fuels and gaseous by-products from the manufacturing sector, particularly those containing sulfur and nitrogen oxides. Once these pollutants and the atmospheric moisture combine, they form acid.

(162)   Quebec is accepted as one of the world's cultural regions because of its:

The correct answer is: (C) Language

Quebec is the only place in the western world where French is the dominant language used by the majority of citizens. Quebec is a province within Canada, where French is recognized as an official language. Only Canada's province of New Brunswick is like Quebec in formally designating French as an official language.

The residents of Quebec also come from very diverse backgrounds, with around 50 ethnic groups having a population of over 10,000 people and around 25 of them having a population of over 4,500 people.

(163)   Advancements in communication that made it easy to convey messages across the globe in seconds involved:

The correct answer is: (B) Satellites used by telecommunications networks

Communication satellites are artificial satellites used in relaying and amplifying telecommunication by radio signals. The person who played the greatest role in designing the world's first artificial satellite was Sergei Korolev, who was the chief designer of the Soviet Sputnik program initiated by the Soviet Union in 1957.

(164) Pittsburgh became a significant center of steel production owing to:

The correct answer is: (B) The city's close proximity to deposits of coal and iron

Pittsburgh, a city in the US state of Pennsylvania, is known for mining. Production of coal in the area rose significantly between 1880 and 1916, with production output in tons increasing from 4.3 million to 40 million.

(165) _____ is likely to succeed in giving people a sense of cultural unity.

The correct answer is: (B) Use of a common language

Research by experts has shown that people are likely to feel more unified when they have a language they can use in common. For one, through the common language people are able to easily learn one another's culture and appreciate it, acquire education together, understand common religions and so on. Owing to these factors, people are less suspicious of one another and develop a sense of oneness.

(166) On the western side of Europe, forests have mainly developed in areas of high elevation because:

The correct answer is: (C) Trees generally do best on steep slopes

The forests in this region of Western Europe can be found in countries like Switzerland and Austria, as well as the Czech Republic, Germany and France.

(167) The Great Lakes were created because of:

The correct answer is: (B)What the glaciers did

The Great Lakes are composed of Lakes Superior, Ontario and Erie, as well as Lakes Michigan and Huron. Formation of these lakes started toward the end of the last glacial era, which was about 14,000 years ago. Ice sheets began to retreat, leaving massive basins behind. These land basins later filled with water after the ice melted. Over the years, these lakes have facilitated transport, trade and fishing, even as they serve as a great animal and plant habitat.

(168)   There are times when El Niño, the warm ocean current, is replaced by the cooler Peru current. This happens along the Peruvian coastline, and as a result, anchovies that seabirds rely on for food decrease. Owing to that shortage of birds, there is a drop in the number of birds left to roost along the Peruvian coastal islands.

This passage tells of the effect El Niño has on the _____ of Peru.

The correct answer is: (C) Ecosystem

El Niño affects ecosystems, sometimes for the good and other times for the worse. In the southern parts of the United States, for instance, El Niño has been found to cause an increase in rainfall, which sometimes becomes excessive and destructive. Also, El Niño can lead to alteration in ocean temperatures, which then has significant impact on marine life.

(169)   One major reason countries choose to become members of international bodies such as the UN is that:

The correct answer is: (B) Many of the problems the world faces affect more than a single country

These organizations create a forum in which different countries can highlight issues that can be solved from a common front.

(170)   The country of Switzerland is situated within a mountain range called:

The correct answer is: (A) The Alps

Switzerland, which is a landlocked country that borders Germany, France, Austria and Italy, is mountainous and sits right within the Alps. On the country's northern side are the Jura Mountains.

(171)   _____ follow a profession that requires them to live in many places.

The correct answer is: (B) Nurses

Owing to the nature of nurses' work, including accompanying doctors and paramedics where medical help is needed, they are prone to moving to different locations without much prior notice. Sometimes they relocate on their own to render services, which may at times take longer than initially anticipated.

The other categories of jobs given as options—miners, technicians and ranchers—are attached to specific locations, so these professionals have to live within or around those locations. Miners live where the mines are, ranchers where their ranches are and technicians where the oil refineries are located.

(172) Most of the towns in ancient Greece were developed on hilltops mainly because:

The correct answer is: (C) It was easier to defend a town on a hilltop than one in a low-lying area

The early Greeks liked to build their towns on hills because they found it easier to keep them protected. Athens is one such example of a town built on elevated land. The Greeks would farm there for subsistence and commerce, but the main reason for establishing the town there was protection from enemies. This was the era when the Roman Empire was being expanded and local wars were common.

(173) Disposal of detergents after use has been found to destabilize _____ natural balance.

The correct answer is: (D) Lakes' and streams'

Pollution of water by chemicals like those found in detergents continues to be a global concern. Many of the detergents in common use have roughly between 35% and 75% of phosphate salts, yet phosphates are known to be a great water pollutant in many ways, one of them being inhibiting biodegradation of organic substances.

(174) _____ contributes greatly to the greenhouse effect.

The correct answer is: (B) Burning of fuels (e.g., gas, oil and coal)

Ordinarily, the trapping of heat within the greenhouse gases causes the Earth to become warmer. The main greenhouse gases that lead to heat entrapment include carbon dioxide, methane and nitrous oxide.

(175)   Which of the countries listed below is farthest south?

The correct answer is: (C) New Zealand

Whereas New Zealand is 40.9°S in latitude, Uruguay is 32.5°S, South Africa 30.6°S and Zaire just 4°S.

(176)   In the late 1800s, one factor that contributed greatly to the expansion of human settlements westwards was:

The correct answer is: (B) The construction of the railway

The railway took over as a means of transport in the United States from steamboats, which had been the major mode of transport for long distances from as early as 1807.

(177)   Based on your geographical knowledge, which statement below is most likely to be true?

The correct answer is: (C) If ships did not use the Panama Canal when coming from San Francisco, the only other route to get to New York would be 13,000 miles long

That route entails sailing all around Cape Horn, a route that became popular in the days of the Gold Rush. Cape Horn is a headland that is rocky, within the southern part of Chile's Tierra del Fuego archipelago.

(178)   Among the cities listed below, which one rates highest in manufacturing and trade?

The correct answer is: (A) Kinshasa in Congo

Companies operating in Kinshasa, Congo, include Heineken, the Vodacom Group, MAG International, Ericsson Worldwide, Nestlé and others. The United Bank of Africa also has a presence there.

(179) The smallest ocean in the world is:

The correct answer is: (B) The Arctic

There are five oceans in the world, and the Arctic is the smallest among them. The other oceans are the Pacific, the Atlantic, the Indian and the Antarctic. The Arctic Ocean measures 14 million square kilometers. While the Arctic is around one and a half times the size of the United States, the largest ocean, the Pacific, is around a third of the size of the Earth.

(180) The state of Florida is a good example of:

The correct answer is: (C) A peninsula

A peninsula is a mass of land that has water on all the sides except for the part that extends from the mainland. In the case of Florida, it is surrounded by the waters of the Atlantic Ocean, and in some parts it borders the Gulf of Mexico. The US states that border Florida are Georgia and Alabama.

(181) Why did early peoples often settle within river valleys?

The correct answer is: (D) The soils in the river valleys were rich because of the deposits that came with floodwaters

Wherever rivers run, they tend to collect debris and rich humus, and these are deposited on riverbanks—especially during floods. That makes areas within river valleys great for growing crops. With the soil rich and moisture in abundance, crops thrive.

(182) One major reason US cities began to build skyscrapers was:

The correct answer is: (C) Land was more intensively and efficiently utilized

Skyscrapers are buildings built to big heights, usually serving to define the skyline of the city. The United States was the first country to begin construction of skyscrapers, and it continues to lead in terms of numbers of skyscrapers built and occupied. In the early days, skyscrapers were meant for commercial purposes, but soon they began to serve as residential buildings. Such buildings are economically beneficial to a country because in many cities, the population grows so fast that the land available for use continues to diminish.

(183) Among the continents listed below, _____ is in the lead with respect to manufacturing and trade.

The correct answer is: (B) Europe

Among the European countries leading the pack with strong economies are France, Italy, Spain, the Netherlands, Switzerland, Sweden, Poland, and Belgium. As for Germany, although it represents the largest economy on the continent, its strength began to dwindle after the reunification of West and East Germany in 1990.

(184) The region highest in elevation in the continent of Africa is:

The correct answer is: (D) The eastern side

Most of Africa's highlands are found in the eastern region, not only in East Africa, but also in areas of eastern Zimbabwe where the country borders Mozambique.

(185) Which of these is a capital city on the African continent?

The correct answer is: (A) Luanda in Angola

Luanda is not only Angola's capital, but it is also the largest of its cities. It is also the country's major port, which leads in industrialization and culture. Luanda as a city, plus its entire metropolitan area, constitutes the city with the biggest population of Portuguese-speaking people the world over.

Angola was a Portuguese colony from 1575. Up to the time the country gained independence in 1975, Luanda was known by its Portuguese name, São Paulo da Assunção de Loanda.

(186) Which of the options below has the highest elevation?

The correct answer is: (A) Lake Titicaca

Lake Titicaca, which is said to be a million years old, has a high elevation, being 3,810 meters above sea level. This lake lies between the South American countries of Bolivia and Peru.

(187) The equator runs across which of the countries listed below?

The correct answer is: (D) Indonesia

Indonesia is a nation composed of several volcanic islands, all within the southeastern part of Asia. It is one of those places where the equator cuts across, so it is not surprising that its climate is tropical. The temperature in its plains along the coast averages 28°C, whereas in the mountainous regions the average is a close 26°C. Nevertheless, humidity is pretty high, between 70% and 90%.

(188) Which step comes first in the process of strategic management?

The correct answer is: (B) Strategy formulation

Strategic management entails planning and monitoring as well as carrying out analysis and assessment, all on a continuous basis. Whatever is done under strategic management is geared toward helping achieve the objectives and goals of the organization. In this endeavor, the very first step is formulation of the strategy. When this is done well, it serves as a guide to the other aspects of the management process.

(189) From the options provided below, choose the one with people who ought to be involved when strategies are being implemented.

The correct answer is: (D) All the people mentioned in options (A) to (C)

All participants, as long as they are responsible, should take part in implementing strategy. This includes the board of directors and the company's main shareholders (especially if it is a public listed company), the CEO and other members within company management.

(190) Lucy traveled from New York to Greece in December 2001 and found a nice blouse that cost 6,274 Drachmas. As per the prevailing exchange rate, one U.S. dollar was equivalent to 200.5 Drachmas. What was the price of the blouse in U.S. dollars?

The correct answer is: (B) $31.29

Cost of blouse = 6,274 drachmas

1 US dollar = 200.5 drachmas

Hence cost of shoe in USD = 6,274 ÷ 200.5 = $31.29

(191) Chef Abdi has a recipe that uses three cups of wheat flour, which is a mixture of both white and brown flour. Three-eighths of the three cups constitutes the white flour. How many cups of brown flour does Abdi need?

The correct answer is: (B) 1.875 cups

3/8 of 3 cups is white flour.

Therefore, the brown flour constitutes 3 cups – (3/8 of 3 cups)

Brown flour = 3 cups – (3/8 of 3 cups) or simply 5/8 of 3 cups

In absolute amounts, white flour = 3/8 of 3 cups = 1.125 cups

White flou½ 1.125 cups and total flour = 3 cups

Therefore, brown flour = 3 cups = 1.125 cups, which is 1.875 cups.

(192) Mary lives 6 1/2 km from the school library. She is able to walk a third of the way without tak½ a rest. What is the distance she must still cove½fter resting?

The correct answer is: (C) 4.33 k½Total distance = 6 1/2 ½Distance cov½d before the rest = 1/3 of 6 1/2 km

Distance to cover after the rest = 2/3 of 6 1/2 km, which is 2/3 x 6 1/2 km

2/3 x 6 1/2 km = 4.33 km

(193) One-fourth of all cars sold by a local dealership are high-end luxury models. The dealership sold 360 cars from that category last year. What is the to¼ number of cars the dealership sold last year?

The correct answer is: (C) 1,440 cars

Let total number of cars sold be x

If¼4x = 360 cars, what is x?

You need to get the unknown on one side alone,¼d the unknown in this case ¼x. T¼4liminate t¼41/4 on the left side, you need to divide both sides of the equal sign with 1/4. You will therefore have:

1/4x ÷ 1/4 = (360 ÷ 1/4) cars

It is standard practice to change the division sign to a multiplication sign while at the same time inverting the fraction you were meant to divide with, to make the calculations easier. In this case you will have:

x = 360 x 4/1, which works out to 1,440 cars.

(194) The number of people who fit in eight subway cars while seated is 400. How many people would fit in five subway cars while seated?

The correct answer is: (B) 250

Let c stand for cars.

If 8c = 400, what is 5c?

Begin by calculating the value of c by working out the equation you have just created: 8c = 400.

Work toward leaving the unknown, c, on one side alone, by dividing either side of the equal sign by 8. You will therefore have:

8c ÷ 8 = 400 ÷ 8

Therefore, c = 50

Now you know that one subway car, or 1c, will fit 50 people.

So, if c = 50, what is 5c?

5c = 5 x 50 = 250 people

[You can also work backwards to check if the value you gave c works for eight subway cars. If c = 50, what is 8c? It is 8 x 50, which works out to 400. Information has already been provided that 8 subway cars fit 400 people, so the value you have given c is correct.]

(195) Jepkosgei ran half a mile within four minutes. If she runs at the same rate, how far will she have run in 15 minutes?

The correct answer is: (A) 1.875 miles

Begin by calculating the distance Jepkosgei runs in one minute at this rate.

4 minutes = 0.5 miles

Therefore, 1 minute = 0.5 miles ÷ 4 = 0.125 mile

So, if she runs 0.125 miles in a minute, in 15 minutes she will have covered:

(15 x 0.125) miles; and this works out to 1.875 miles.

(196) If you have a rope 10 feet long and you want to cut it into 8-inch-long segments, how many of those pieces will you have?

The correct answer is: (C) 15 pieces

When working with items that are given in different units of measurement, the first step should be to convert the units so that you will be working with like terms. This problem calls for dividing, so it should be more convenient to work with smaller units; converting feet to inches.

How many inches are there in a foot? There are 12 inches.

So 10 feet = 10 x 12 inches = 120 inches.

When you cut segments that are 8 inches long from a length of 120 inches, you get:

120 inches ÷ 8 inches = 15

Hence, a 10-foot rope cut into 8-inch segments produces 15 equal pieces.

(197) A reputable restaurant pays a tip of 15% on the bill after 6% tax has been charged. If the bill before tax and tip totals $38.40, what is the amount of the tip in dollars?

The correct answer is: (A) $6.10

Begin by calculating the amount of tax in dollars:

6% of $38.40, which is $2.30.

This means the tip should be charged on $(38.40+2.30), or $40.70.

Since the tip is charged at 15% of the bill after tax, the amount of tip will be:

15% of $40.70 = $6.10

(198) For a certain company, cab charges for the initial mile total $3, and for every additional half mile the charge is $1. If Asha takes a cab ride for 10 miles, how much is she supposed to pay?

The correct answer = (D) $21

Put aside $3 for the very first mile. Now you have 9 miles remaining and you have so far pa½$3. Every half mile after the first one mile costs $1, and this is the rate you need to use on the 9 remaining miles.

So if 1/2 mile = $1, how much will 9 miles cost? The simplest calculation would be to find out first the cost of 1 mile, which should be: $1 x 2 because 1 mile equals 2 half miles. Since $1 x 2 = $2, meaning 1 mile costs $2, it means 9 miles should cost $2 x 9.

$2 x 9 = $18; and once you add the cost of the first mile the total becomes:

$18 + $3 = $21.

(199) An overseas automobile manufacturer pays $3 in shipping charges for every 1 kilogram of automobile parts sent to the United States. If the cargo sent weighs 200 pounds, how much should the manufacturer pay when rounded to the nearest dollar? Take the ratio of pound to kilogram to be 1:0.455.

The correct answer is: (D) $273

How many kilograms are there in 200 pounds? They should be:

200 pounds ÷ 0.455, which is equal to 200 x 455/1,000 = 91 kg. In short, the weight of the cargo shipped is 200 pounds, or 91 kg.

Since 1 kg costs $3, 91 kg should cost $(91 x 3) = $273.

(200) John spent $25 after dining in a city restaurant. He noted that the bill before tip added was $21. Roughly what percentage tip did John leave?

The correct answer is: (B) 19%

Amount of tip was $25 - $21 = $4.

To find the percentage tip John left, you need to divide $4 by John's initial expenditure, $21. $4 ÷ $21 = 19%.

Test 2: Questions

(1) What major role does the board of directors play?

(A) Representing the shareholders

(B) Protecting its self-interests

(C) Providing oversight on behalf of the CEO

(D) Ensuring quarterly projections are attained

(2) Which of the statements listed below explains what differentiates a vision statement from a mission statement?

(A) Both statements mean the same thing

(B) The vision statement is more precise

(C) The guidelines provided by the mission statement are more pragmatic than those the vision statement provides

(D) The vision statement does not necessarily address matters related to the company

(3) If a grocery store franchise decides to buy out several farms in your locality and starts farming so it can grow its own supplies, the strategy this franchise will have implemented is referred to as:

(A) Synergistic integration

(B) Backward integration

(C) Horizontal integration

(D) Forward integration

(4) Which of the options below does not automatically lead to increased competition among companies?

(A) Slow industrial growth

(B) Having several competitors with roughly the same strength

(C) High overhead costs

(D) Industry deregulation

(5) Which of the business strategies listed below depends on production that has to be adjusted in order to satisfy immediate demand in the market and bring down costs linked to idle time for employees and facilities?

(A) Production that is streamlined

(B) Production done on a just-in-time basis

(C) Production done on a last-in first-out basis

(D) Industrial production

(6) Which of the options listed below does not exemplify strong infrastructure that provides a competitive advantage?

(A) Officers of a company working hand in hand with key customers to seal a deal

(B) Cost reduction through implementation of efficient IT systems

(C) People involved in negotiations in order to maintain a positive relationship with industry regulators

(D) The marketing department helping the company penetrate an entirely new market

(7) One way you can tell when a company is able to meet its short-term obligations is:

(A) Its level of liquidity

(B) Its leverage

(C) Its productivity

(D) Its profitability

(8) One reason a software company might have a market value that's larger than its book value is:

(A) The market includes the company's intellectual property in its overall value

(B) Technology firms use methods of accounting that vary from the ones used by traditional firms

(C) Software was given the wrong pricing

(D) This is just hype, as such a situation is not possible

(9) In order for a company to alleviate high turnover of staff within a competitive industry, the company should:

(A) Reduce the amount of money spent on HR, considering most employees are determined to leave

(B) Make the workplace more competitive

(C) Increase efforts to recruit more staff

(D) Introduce programs geared toward retaining employees

(10) Who is involved in employee evaluation during a 360° evaluation process?

(A) Subordinates

(B) Colleagues

(C) Managers

(D) Subordinates, colleagues and managers

(11) During the past decade or so, modern IT systems have had significant impact on some aspects of business. Choose one aspect below that has been most impacted.

(A) Removal of distractions affecting employees at the workplace

(B) Reduction of negative interactions among fellow workers

(C) Increase in social capital

(D) Restriction of social network growth at the workplace

(12) Which of the qualities listed below is not a good leadership characteristic?

(A) Being self-motivated

(B) Being focused on goals

(C) Being detail-oriented

(D) Being reactive

(13) Which of the answers listed below details a failure that is common in businesses that are barely able to keep up with their daily functions?

(A) Failure to do an objective analysis of business operations

(B) Failure to keep reevaluating strategic objectives

(C) Failure to critique any basic assumptions made regarding the prevailing business environment

(D) Each of the failures listed above

(14) Which of the activities listed below is not a management technique referred to as "management by walking around"?

(A) Being open to fresh ideas and not being argumentative

(B) Having set questions for particular people to respond to

(C) Wandering through the business premises without any particular plan in mind

(D) Letting staff and others guide the conversations you partake in

(15) The relationship that should exist between a corporate structure and strategy is:

(A) Corporate structure designed to enable implementation of the corporate strategy

(B) Corporate strategy and corporate structure developed independently

(C) Designing corporate strategy with the corporate structure in mind

(D) None

(16) What is one of the advantages associated with the corporate structure of a holding company?

(A) Reduction of overhead costs and those related to personnel, enabled by the small size of the corporation's office

(B) Integration of divisions that enhances efficiency and reduces costs

(C) Executives being aware of the decisions being made at all company levels

(D) Executives having immense control over the company's day-to-day operations

(17) What is one of the risks of outsourcing?

(A) Flexibility of personnel being reduced

(B) Loss of critical skills

(C) Loss of nonessential skills

(D) Reduction of personnel cost

(18) When a company is faced with a challenging business environment, the best way to proceed is:

(A) Set vague goals for maximum flexibility

(B) Write detailed plans in order to cover all business possibilities

(C) Avoid milestones in order to let the workflow be fluid

(D) Innovate controls for strategic purposes, which are suitable for the prevailing environment

(19) Which of these things is not associated with setting short-term goals?

(A) Setting attainable goals

(B) Emphasizing best performance

(C) Defining specific timelines within which to complete a project

(D) Clearly laying out standards against which to measure success

(20)   Emphasizing corporate culture and offering intangible rewards becomes very useful when:

(A) The work being performed is of a creative nature and requires self-direction

(B) The work being done is already standardized

(C) The tasks being performed require low skills and are of a repetitive nature

(D) The measurement and evaluation of the work being performed is precise

(21) One major difference between a joint venture and a strategic alliance is that:

(A) Whereas those involved in a joint venture are legally bound, those involved in a strategic alliance are not

(B) Whereas you can have only two companies in a joint venture, there can be several companies in a strategic alliance

(C) In a joint venture, a third-party entity must be created

(D) It is easy to accuse a strategic alliance of fixing prices illegally but that is not the case for a joint venture

(22)   It is reasonable for stockholders to expect company managers to:

(A) Make their investment more valuable

(B) Minimize the risk stockholders are exposed to

(C) Maximize stockholders' short-term gains

(D) Keep diversifying the portfolio of every stockholder

(23)   A company should consider undertaking vertical integration when:

(A) It is important to reduce the costs of transacting and improve coordination

(B) The company is not liquid

(C) Two or more companies that specialize differently are merging

(D) A company cannot increase its profits within its value chain segment

(24)   When you have a company's head office continuously advising its subsidiaries, this is referred to as:

(A) Centralizing

(B) Parenting

(C) Mentoring

(D) Consolidating

(25) Among the options listed below, which represents a strategic alliance that is not wise for a business?

(A) A company maintaining clear communication with its strategic partners

(B) Making expectations clear among all alliance members

(C) Ensuring fair treatment of every partner

(D) Relying on documents for governing to ensure the smooth running of the venture

(26) Every company hopes to be in a position to earn beyond normal profits. What is the meaning of "normal profits"?

(A) Any profit is normal profit

(B) A return that enables a business to cover risk and remain in business

(C) A return earned the previous year plus the percentage of inflation

(D) A business cost that adds up to a small amount of money

(27) One of the required factors for a market to be deemed mature is:

(A) Low rate of growth and high intensity of competition

(B) Low rate of growth with plenty of room to expand in the future

(C) High rate of growth and ease of entry into the market

(D) A product design that determines profit more than the efficiency of business

(28)   The literacy rate in the United States was greatly impacted by a change instituted at the national level in the 1800s. What change was it?

(A) Making education compulsory

(B) Banning slavery

(C) Building railroads

(D) Expanding the US territory

(29)   What significant role do syndicates in the news industry play?

(A) They offer collective bargaining power for editors through their capacity to organize

(B) They are involved in operation of chain newspapers

(C) They gather and sell work compiled by journalists and photographers as well as other contributors en masse

(D) They control the media in particular regions

(30)   In the late 1800s, magazines reduced their prices in a drastic way. What caused that big drop in magazine prices?

(A) Introduction of printing in color

(B) A rise in revenues from advertising

(C) Economic deflation

(D) A drop in postal delivery fees

(31) Muckraking is:

(A) Writing false stories for political reasons

(B) Incorporating unnecessary matters in news writing just to embarrass certain politicians

(C) Provoking particular individuals or groups of people so they take action

(D) Covering stories of a risqué nature regarding celebrities

(32) The first time radio was used as a major medium for dissemination of news was:

(A) In WWII

(B) During the 1890s

(C) In WWI

(D) During the Cold War

(33) What is meant by a "pseudo-event"?

(A) A reenacted real event

(B) An event designed specifically to garner publicity

(C) An inconsequential event given much limelight on a day when news is slow

(D) A fake event designed to be picked up by cameras

(34)   The 1938 Foreign Agents Registration Act's target was Ivy Lee, a pioneer in public relations. What did he do to prompt the enactment of that law?

(A) Wrote about the Great Depression

(B) Denounced WWII

(C) Represented Germany during the Nazi regime

(D) Renounced his own citizenship

(35)   When professionals in public relations perform their work, their target audiences are:

(A) The public in general

(B) Shareholders

(C) The employees

(D) Employees, shareholders and the public in general

(36)   The function of public affairs differs from that of public relations in that:

(A) The professionals in public affairs mostly have the media to deal with

(B) The professionals in public affairs solely have the public to deal with

(C) The professionals in public affairs work with influential institutions on behalf of their company

(D) The professionals in public affairs are government employees

(37) The standard unit used to express the efficiency of a given advertisement is:

(A) Cost per household

(B) Cost per thousand

(C) Cost per million

(D) Cost per hundred

(38) What is the correct meaning of a paradigm?

(A) The entire knowledge body in a particular context

(B) A particular theory responsible for organizing information pertaining to the world

(C) The process responsible for determining the way people take in information

(D) A given strategic plan

(39) The mass communication theory of two-step flow can be summarized as:

(A) Ideas keep flowing from makers of opinions to followers of opinions

(B) People are willing to accommodate just two fresh ideas at one time

(C) It takes a process of two steps to persuade people to embrace fresh ideas

(D) Fresh ideas must, of necessity, emerge from two varying sources for them to be taken as believable

(40)   Klapper's reinforcement theory of mass media is that:

(A) It can effectively alter political paradigms

(B) It can effectively form bold, fresh ideas

(C) The power it has can reinforce only beliefs that already exist

(D) It can effectively change social norms or customs

(41) Which of the options below exemplifies setting an agenda?

(A) An editor chooses to print on the first page of the newspaper a story that can politically embarrass someone

(B) A company decides to place an advertisement with a particular newspaper

(C) A writer decides to paraphrase a particular interview

(D) A photographer decides to retain some photographs and not others

(42)   What is the theory that holds that media creates an image that is accepted only because people make a choice to believe that image?

(A) Social construct theory

(B) Dependency theory

(C) Theory of critical communication

(D) Cultivation theory

(43)   Companies that deal with polling normally seek public opinion using:

(A) Sampling

(B) Experimentation

(C) Interpolation

(D) Trial and error

(44)   Modern-day presidential campaigns tend to put their focus primarily on _____ because of being influenced by the media.

(A) The various backgrounds of the candidates

(B) The varying personalities of the candidates

(C) The experience candidates have with foreign policy

(D) Social policies

(45)   Which of the options below provides an accurate description of libel?

(A) Reporting that is false and malicious and causes damage to a person's reputation

(B) Reporting of any kind that causes damage to a person's reputation

(C) The First Amendment protects people from libel

(D) "Libel" is a term used only in print media

(46)   Sometimes the question of whether or not a source of information should be shielded arises. Is it the right of a journalist to shield or protect a source of confidential information?

(A) Yes, the journalist ought to shield the source unless that person has broken a certain law

(B) That depends on which US state the issue has arisen in

(C) Yes, in any case, the Federal Shield law protects the journalist

(D) That is dependent on the specific information the source has provided

(47)   Which country spearheaded the initiation of Radio Free Europe?

(A) The Union of Soviet Socialist Republics

(B) Germany

(C) France

(D) The United States

(48)   Whenever someone close to you nods in the middle of a conversation as you speak, it exemplifies:

(A) Providing feedback during personal communication

(B) Unique encoding

(C) Generation of noise during mass communication

(D) Generation of noise during personal communication

(49)   There is a well-known statement Marshall McLuhan made, which is, "The medium is the message." The meaning of this statement is that:

(A) It is inconsequential what medium is used in conveying an idea

(B) People are more concerned about the medium being used than the particular content being delivered

(C) The media has the capacity to control people's thinking in a direct manner

(D) It is essential to select the appropriate medium through which to communicate your ideas

(50)   Which of the options below exemplifies technological determinism?

(A) Shifting from subscribing to the conventional newspaper to an online one

(B) Signing up to open a personal email account

(C) Believing that society will break down specifically because of the internet

(D) Disposing of your conventional landline and relying solely on your cell phone

(51) The very first form of media to be mass-produced was:

(A) Books

(B) The radio

(C) Newspapers

(D) Music records

(52) Which of the options below best defines "literacy"?

(A) The capacity to carry out interaction among members of society

(B) The capacity to make use of a particular medium

(C) The capacity to verbalize words

(D) The capacity to read sentences that are not complex

(53) How can "genre" best be defined?

(A) Grouped works that consumers ordinarily enjoy

(B) A particular story arc writers are prone to following

(C) Grouped works in a particular medium, sharing several conventions

(D) A category of writers who like similar topics

(54) The voting trend or behavior people adopt is mostly influenced by:

(A) The information they read online

(B) Televised news

(C) The information they read in print media

(D) Conversations they have with their friends

(55) What is meant by the "CNN effect"?

(A) The power televised media has in setting the agenda

(B) The influence the 24-hour news cycle has on politics

(C) The influence the 24-hour news cycle has on different media channels

(D) The power media has in simplifying news stories

(56)   When the government first began regulating radio and TV broadcasts, it gave the justification that:

(A) It was necessary to regulate commerce between states

(B) Transmissions posed a threat to people's health

(C) Airwaves were scarce

(D) There was a need to protect citizens

(57) What does the "Fairness Doctrine" mean?

(A) It is an FCC policy stating that it is compulsory for broadcasters to air all perspectives equally

(B) It is a doctrine regulating broadcasting rights near US borders

(C) It is the doctrine that bars media from broadcasting political matters a short while before an election

(D) It is the FCC policy stating that radio broadcasts should be open to being heard by any person

(58)   In a recession, the opinion of Keynesians is that the government:

(A) Should increase its spending

(B) Should ensure inflation keeps rising

(C) Should lower taxes

(D) Should cut its spending

(59) Which of the options below matches a renowned economist to the wrong influential work?

(A) J. M. Keynes – *The General Theory of Employment, Interest and Money*

(B) Milton Friedman – *The Return of Depression Economics*

(C) Karl Marx – *Capital*

(D) Adam Smith – *The Wealth of Nations*

(60) There are some countries whose Gini indices are high. What is also true of those countries?

(A) A lot of wealth is concentrated within a tiny section of society

(B) Their standard of living is seen as high

(C) Gender equality in those countries is impressively high

(D) They are set to meet the Millennium Development Goals set by the UN

(61) When calculating the GDP of the United States, _____ is omitted.

(A) Salaries earned by US residents who are not US citizens

(B) Money a company from Italy spends while operating in the United States

(C) Profit earned by a Brazil-based company whose owner is a US citizen

(D) Money spent by the US government

(62) At an all-you-can-eat buffet, John hungrily eats his first full plate, fills a second one and enjoys it, but then realizes that, as much as he would like to, he cannot possibly eat a third plate. Choose one option from those listed below that explains this the way an economist would.

(A) The marginal utility of the food has decreased

(B) The marginal cost of the food has increased

(C) The total utility of the food has decreased

(D) The food supply curve has increased

(63) In macroeconomics, efficiency is best described as:

(A) Maximizing total utility through allocation of resources

(B) Matching supply with demand as closely as possible

(C) Matching marginal utility and marginal cost as closely as possible

(D) Reducing cost as much as possible

(64) Market failure is said to happen when:

(A) A product has no demand

(B) A trader does not make money

(C) Resources are not efficiently allocated by the market

(D) Goods can be neither bought nor sold

(65)   When a government prints a large amount of money, what effect does that commonly bring about?

(A) There is more wealth in that nation because there is more money

(B) Prices in this currency rise

(C) There is an increase in the overall liquidity of the nation

(D) More savings are made in that currency

(66)   Why would company X contract with company Y to produce shirts if company X does a better job both at producing the shirts and selling them compared to company Y?

(A) Company X sees potential benefits from future competition

(B) Because of company Y's absolute advantage in producing the shirts

(C) Company X does not need to contract with company Y

(D) Because of company Y's comparative advantage in producing the shirts

(67)   What is the equilibrium price of a product?

(A) The production cost of the product

(B) The price point where demand and supply are equal

(C) The cost per unit excluding overhead cost

(D) The price equal to the product's inherent value

(68)   Marginal costs of manufactured goods decrease as the production volume goes up. Why does that happen?

(A) There is more efficiency in the factory

(B) New workers are okay with receiving lower wages

(C) Fixed cost can be spread out over many more units

(D) To cover decreased marginal utility

(69)   What is likely to happen when government controls prices on wheat but the cost of production of the wheat exceeds the imposed price?

(A) The wheat sellers lose money

(B) A wheat shortage will be experienced

(C) The wheat sellers experience a growth in profits

(D) Retailers buy wheat from sellers at a lower market value

(70)   What causes the difference between short-term and long-term effects brought about by demand change?

(A) Markets first watch to see whether it is a permanent change

(B) Markets take time to understand the changes

(C) Situations that affect equilibrium take a while to settle

(D) Adjusting to a market involves a certain cost

(71) Which of these statements best describes digital information?

(A) Information you can access online

(B) Information you can read from the screen of a computer

(C) Information recorded under discrete data

(D) Information you find stored on computers

(72)   Which of the statements below is false about the advantages of LCD monitors over CRT monitors?

(A) LCD monitors use less space

(B) An LCD monitor is cheaper

(C) LCD monitors have screens that are flat

(D) LCD monitors do not distort images at the edges

(73)   How was the floppy disk named?

(A) It got its name because of the bendable nature of the disks

(B) It got its name because the disks are placed between computers

(C) It got its name because you can easily change the data

(D) It got its name because some consider its encoding protocol to be sloppy

(74)   What makes random access memory (RAM) random?

(A) Data is stored in random places

(B) It randomly searches for data

(C) It is not exactly random, but RAM is able to gain access to any given data point at any given time

(D) It has a somewhat random total capacity

(75) What is the role of the BIOS?

(A) It acts as the mediator between the computer and the OS

(B) It is responsible for loading the OS

(C) It acts as the mediator between the user and the OS

(D) It is used when the OS fails

(76)   What is the importance of a central processing unit cache?

(A) The size of the cache dictates how many programs the CPU is able to interact with

(B) The size of the cache dictates how many threads the CPU is able to handle

(C) The absence of a cache will cause the CPU to miss many clock cycles

(D) The CPU is able to hold only a single number singly in the absence of a cache

(77) Which of the choices below describes the main limitation found in backward-compatible systems?

(A) When old programs run, they run poorly

(B) New programs are better than old programs

(C) New programs and old programs have frequent runtime conflicts

(D) Backward-compatible systems must be highly complex

(78) What does Moore's law state?

(A) Every five years, computer power triples

(B) Every two years, processing speed doubles

(C) Every one and a half years, memory cost is reduced by half

(D) There is a 10% increase in computer access every year

(79) When you use a computer with no graphics card, what is likely to happen?

(A) It will not be possible for the computer to show 3D graphics

(B) There will not be any images

(C) The computer will not play videos

(D) The system will be very slow

(80) Which of these does not represent malware?

(A) Trojan horses

(B) Adware

(C) Computer virus

(D) Your system being accessed by a hacker

(81) Which process below is not managed by the OS?

(A) Maintaining interoperability

(B) Process management

(C) Memory management

(D) File management

(82) Which of the options below is not an algorithm?

(A) A meal recipe

(B) A computer program

(C) Software documentation

(D) A standard cryptographic attack

(83) Which of these is the least complex algorithm?

(A) Exhaustive search

(B) Dynamic programming

(C) Greedy method

(D) Search for enumeration

(84) Which of the statements below explains how prototyping works in the software engineering field?

(A) A prototype is not a code but the logic of a program

(B) A rough and approximate version that shows proof of concept is quickly designed

(C) A shorter and simpler version that shows proof of concept is designed

(D) Software is designed to solve less difficult problems that are similar

(85) Why is C considered one of the lower-level languages in programming?

(A) It is less powerful compared to other languages

(B) The programmer is able to directly control hardware and memory

(C) It is used to perform only simple tasks

(D) A programmer learns about it in the early stages of programming

(86) Define an object in object-oriented programming.

(A) A data field or data set and the associated methods

(B) Any of the data set the program operates on

(C) A function that can be called on by the program

(D) A part of hardware that has to interact with the program

(87) Which of these describes one of the main advantages in cloud computing?

(A) There is more efficient use of resources

(B) It is more secure

(C) It is easier to design cloud computing programs

(D) The processing power used by programs is less

(88) What is the difference between protocol and algorithm?

(A) Problems are not necessarily solved by protocols

(B) Protocols include more than just one actor

(C) Algorithms indicate what should be done, while protocols also indicate who should do it

(D) Protocols are specifically used in the field of software engineering

(89) Between public key encryption and private key encryption, which is mostly used in modern encryption?

(A) Private key encryption

(B) Public key encryption

(C) Both types of encryption keys are used

(D) Neither of the two key encryptions is used

(90) Why is JPEG format considered lossy?

(A) File markers can easily be lost

(B) There is a loss of data when compressing

(C) The word "lossy" is programming jargon for algorithms used by JPEG

(D) The picture can be rendered useless when the encoding is lost

(91) What dictates an Ethernet network's maximum size?

(A) Ethernet networks do not have a maximum size

(B) The collision domain

(C) How strong the transmitter is

(D) The processing power of the server

(92) Which computer network is the internet considered to have originated from?

(A) FTP

(B) ARPANET

(C) HTTP

(D) The World Wide Web

(93) Which agency regulates IP addresses?

(A) Every company maintains its own IP addresses

(B) ICANN

(C) WWW

(D) It is done by regional registries

(94) Describe open-source software.

(A) Free software

(B) Software that works on any OS

(C) Software developed by nonprofit organizations

(D) Software that has a source code that is freely available

(95)   What is the major disadvantage to relational databases?

(A) You must determine data tags in advance

(B) You must know the relationship between data sets

(C) The presence of redundant data

(D) There is a restriction in the uses of the database

(96)   What activity is responsible for reducing a large amount of data into smaller, meaningful sets of data that can be used?

(A) Data silos

(B) Data mining

(C) SQL querying

(D) Data warehousing

(97)   Define re-identification in online security.

(A) Requiring users to log in again after their session expires

(B) Validating the identity of a user before allowing them to access secure content

(C) Using anonymous information to determine the actual identity of a user

(D) Using secure sessions to validate the identity of a user

(98)   What does error encoding mean?

(A) A code that corrects errors that occur during a routine operation

(B) A type of copy prevention that creates errors intentionally to establish authenticity

(C) Mistakes that are made when writing computer programs

(D) Errors that are made when writing data onto memory

(99)   Describe white-hat hackers.

(A) They are law-abiding security experts

(B) They are hackers employed by the government

(C) They expose vulnerabilities in cyber security so that those vulnerabilities can be fixed

(D) They are programmers whose role is to hunt down cybercriminals

(100)   Which of the options below can be part of metadata in a document?

(A) How frequently a document is visited

(B) When the document was created

(C) Usernames of all the people who have had access to a document

(D) All of the above

(101)   In the sentence below, which section do you think needs editing for incorrect grammar, incorrect spelling, wordiness or inappropriate choice of words?

According to her report, a ten year old girl helped the injured man by the roadside.

(A) A *ten year old girl*

(B) *According to her report*

(C) *Helped the injured man*

(D) *By the roadside*

(102) What action will help improve the sentence below?

Remember to fix the leaking roof when you get home, you might get into trouble when it rains again.

(A) Change to third person

(B) Fix parallelism

(C) Correct the comma fault

(D) Use commas on parenthetical remarks

(103) What action will improve the sentence below?

If they would have put all their money in that bank, they would be penniless now that the bank went under.

(A) Eliminating the tense shift

(B) Fix parallelism

(C) Fix comma splice

(D) Fix subject-verb agreement

(104) Which action will improve the sentence below?

After intense training, the girl's football team scored their first goal in two years.

(A) Change intense to hard

(B) Replace the comma with a semicolon

(C) Replace *their* with *its*

(D) Change the modifier

(105)   Which action will best improve the sentence below?

The engine was washed before leaving the garage in case the impure oil had settled at the bottom of the engine.

(A) Change *had settled* to *settle*

(B) Use active voice

(C) Correct tense shift

(D) Correct subject-verb agreement

(106)   Which action will best improve the sentence below?

Lying on the wet grass, Lisa found her lost diamond necklace.

(A) Discard the comma

(B) Discard the tense shift

(C) Fix the parallelism

(D) Fix misplaced modifiers

(107)   Which action best improves the sentence below?

The three triplets had a lovely time at the top-notch hotel.

(A) Discard *three*

(B) Fix the parallelism

(C) Correct the subject-verb agreement

(D) Eliminate the hyphen used in *top-notch*

(108)   Which action will improve the sentence below?

The beautiful song, that featured in the Lion King *film, was composed by Travis.*

(A) Eliminate commas

(B) Fix the change in tense

(C) Use a conjunction

(D) Change *composed*

(109)   Which action best improves the sentence below?

The dress which I wore to the party needed to be stitched because I ran a hole through it.

(A) Separate the sentence into two

(B) Add a comma right after *stitched*

(C) Use *that* instead of *which*

(D) Correct misplaced modifiers

(110)   Which action will improve the sentence below?

Torn and weary, Linda decided to buy new office chairs.

(A) Eliminate the comma

(B) Change *chairs* to *couches*

(C) Place the modifier in the right position

(D) Replace *torn*

(111)   Which of the actions below will best improve this sentence?

He couldn't get to see the skit because he had a task to complete.

(A) Correct the modifier that is misplaced

(B) Capitalize *skit*

(C) Correct subject-verb agreement

(D) Use *could not see* instead of *couldn't get to see*

(112)   Which action will improve the sentence below?

There was a large amount of tourists visiting the Preston Museum on a daily basis.

(A) Replace *amount* with *number*

(B) Use *everyday* instead of *daily*

(C) Use a lowercase *m* in *museum*

(D) Use a lowercase *p* in *Preston*

(113)   Which action will best improve the sentence below?

Despite his seemingly generous nature, his deeds were, at the end of the day, self-indulgent.

(A) Eliminate the commas

(B) Fix the modifier

(C) Get rid of the hyphen in *self-indulgent*

(D) Use *actions* instead of *deeds*

(114)   How can you define liquidity trap?

(A) When a company puts too much focus on liquidity and its growth slows down

(B) When instability is caused by insufficient liquidity within a given system

(C) When a problem of cash flow arises following the draining of apparent assets

(D) When individuals with disposable income refuse to invest as they await a drop in prices

(115)   How is stagflation best explained?

(A) An economy that is not only stagnant but also has escalating inflation

(B) An economy with declining employment growth as well as declining inflation

(C) An economy with increasing deflation; a straight contrast to hyperinflation

(D) An economy with changing prices that cause neither deflation nor inflation

(116)   What is the government's way of measuring inflation?

(A) It assesses the changing value of a wide range of wages and salaries

(B) It seeks the opinions of renowned economists

(C) It assesses the changing value of a wide range of values

(D) It assesses the changing value of the American dollar and treasury bonds

(117)   Is it possible to have per capita income go up as median income goes down?

(A) Yes, and there is no relationship between the two measurements

(B) Yes, and it signifies increasing inequality

(C) No, whenever there is per capita income going up in an economy, median income has to rise as well

(D) Yes, and it signifies increasing unemployment

(118)   A factory has been producing 1,000 units of a product, but now management has decided to produce 1,001 units of that same product. What best describes the cost of producing the extra unit?

(A) Expenditure per single unit

(B) The cost of growth

(C) The marginal cost

(D) The cost of overhead

(119)   Select the action that correctly modifies the following statement:

Windstorms are an "every day" occurrence in most of the Northwest United States.

(A) Eliminate the dangling modifier

(B) Rewrite *windstorms* as *wind storms*

(C) Rewrite *every day* as *everyday*

(D) Rewrite *Northwest* as *north west*

(120)   Select the action that correctly modifies the following statement:

Joe Thomas is one of the NFL quarterbacks who has won more than one Super Bowl.

(A) Correct the parallel structure

(B) Place a comma immediately after *quarterbacks*

(C) Replace *has* with *have*

(D) Lowercase *Super Bowl*

(121)   Select the action that correctly modifies the following statement:

She was honest, hardworking and a regular customer at the nearby pub.

(A) Rewrite *hardworking* as *hard working*

(B) Rewrite *nearby* as *neighborhood*

(C) Place a comma immediately after *hardworking*

(D) Correct the parallel structure

(122)   Select the action that correctly modifies the following statement:

The current senator was scared of not retaining his seat; he used a no-holes-barred method during the campaign.

(A) Replace the semicolon with a colon

(B) Uppercase *senator*

(C) Replace *no-holes-barred* with *no-holds-barred*

(D) Eliminate hyphens from *no-holes-barred*

(123) Select the action that correctly modifies the following statement:

When the Johnsons's family car was broken into, the radio was stolen and the window broken.

(A) Replace *Johnsons's* with *Johnsons'*

(B) Correct the subject-verb agreement

(C) Correct the parallel structure

(D) Rewrite the sentence in past-perfect tense.

(124) Select the action that correctly modifies the following statement:

Despite not being able to buy the brand-new Cadillac, Chris was able to go on a test drive with the Cadillac after convincing the dealer to allow him.

(A) Replace the comma with a semicolon

(B) Replace *test drive* with *test-drive*

(C) Interchange the first clause with the last clause

(D) Lowercase *Cadillac*

(125) Select the action that correctly modifies the following statement:

Completing a marathon is an impressive fete regardless of how long it takes.

(A) Replace *regardless* with *irregardless*

(B) Replace the comma with a semicolon

(C) Correct the misplaced modifier

(D) Replace *fete* with *feat*

(126)   Select the action that correctly modifies the following statement:

The Republican Party has particularly strong supporters in the southern state.

(A) Correct the subject/verb agreement

(B) Uppercase *southern*

(C) Replace *has* with *have*

(D) Insert a hyphen between *particularly* and *strong*

(127)   Select the action that correctly modifies the following statement:

After canceling the appointment at the last moment, he felt badly, but he didn't have enough time to make it at the expected time.

(A) Replace *badly* with *bad*

(B) Replace *canceling* with *cancelling*

(C) Replace *at* with *in*

(D) Eliminate *but*

(128)   Select the action that correctly modifies the following statement:

The streets were frozen over, the paths were extremely slippery.

(A) Insert a hyphen between *extremely* and *slippery*

(B) Replace had *frozen* with *froze*

(C) Correct the comma splice

(D) Replace *were* with *are*

(129)   Select the action that correctly modifies the following statement:

The new CEO of the company had large future plans, but the board was adverse to changing too quickly.

(A) Eliminate the comma

(B) Replace *CEO* with *C.E.O.*

(C) Replace *adverse* with *averse*

(D) Replace *quickly* with *fast*

(130)   Select the action that correctly modifies the following statement:

Whoever will be selected for the scholarship will be entitled to four years of full tuition.

(A) Replace *whoever* with *whomever*

(B) Replace *four* with *4*

(C) Eliminate *of*

(D) Insert a hyphen in *four years*

(131)   Select the action that correctly modifies the following statement:

A group of people have demanded an end to the US boycott on Cuban goods.

(A) Lowercase *Cuban*

(B) Emphasize *boycott* by switching the statement to passive voice

(C) Uppercase *goods*

(D) Replace *boycott* with *embargo*

(132)   Select the action that correctly modifies the following statement:

Neither party was completely satisfied with the judgment made by the mediator, but they nonetheless complied.

(A) Replace *mediator* with *arbitrator*

(B) Replace *judgment* with *judgement*

(C) Replace *nonetheless* with *irregardless*

(D) Replace *neither* with *none*

(133)   Select the action that correctly modifies the following statement:

The daughters requested that their father take a break from his work and accompany them to the mall so that they could meet some of they're friends.

(A) Replace *break* with *brake*

(B) Add a comma immediately following *mall*

(C) Replace *they're* with *their*

(D) Add a semicolon after *mall*

(134)   Select the action that correctly modifies the following statement:

After spending three hours in traffic to get to the trendy restaurant, John intended to stay for awhile.

(A) Eliminate the comma that comes after *trendy*

(B) Eliminate *for*

(C) Correct the misplaced modifier

(D) Eliminate the comma after *restaurant*

(135) Select the action that correctly modifies the following statement:

Due to HR bureaucracy, it had become impossible to establish whose responsible for late paychecks.

(A) Replace *paychecks* with *pay checks*

(B) Replace *bureaucratic* with *beureaucratic*

(C) Eliminate *that*

(D) Replace *whose* with *who was*

(136) Select the action that correctly modifies the following statement:

The moment it was discovered that the hedge fund carried out some dirty deals, the SEC dispatched an auditor to pour over the company books.

(A) Replace *pour* with *pore*

(B) Uppercase *hedge fund*

(C) Replace the comma with a semicolon

(D) Replace *auditor* with *adjudicator*

(137) Select the action that correctly modifies the following statement:

The audience was tricked into believing that the hero had died towards the end of the film.

(A) Add a comma after *tricked*

(B) Replace *towards* with *toward*

(C) Replace *is* with *has been*

(D) Eliminate *that*

(138) Select the action that correctly modifies the following statement:

The board of directors are still pondering over whether to release more bonds. Nonetheless, the company still needs more liquidity.

(A) Capitalize each word in *the board of directors*

(B) Replace the semicolon with a comma

(C) Add a conjunction immediately following the semicolon

(D) Replace *are* with *is*

(139) Select the action that correctly modifies the following statement:

The rule of law, a middle class that is developing and free elections are all crucial to a vibrant, functional democracy.

(A) Replace *are* with *is*

(B) Insert a hyphen in *middle class*

(C) Delete *all*

(D) Correct the parallel statement

(140) Select the action that correctly modifies the following statement:

Some parts of the country continue to operate without daylight savings time.

(A) Uppercase *daylights savings*

(B) Replace *savings* with *saving*

(C) Replace *operate* with *operates*

(D) Insert a hyphen in *daylight savings*

(141)   Select the action that correctly modifies the following statement:

The board constitutes eleven individuals from departments across the company committee.

(A) Delete *department*

(B) Replace *constitutes* with *comprises*

(C) Replace *individuals* with *people*

(D) Replace *committee* with *commitee*

(142)   Select the action that correctly modifies the following statement:

The novel affected great personal growth in my years as a teenager, so I've recommended it to a number of teens ever since.

(A) Replace the semicolon with a comma

(B) Replace *number* with *amount*

(C) Replace *teenager* with *teen-ager*

(D) Replace *affected* with *effected*

(143)   Select the action that correctly modifies the following statement:

As soon as the closed-door meeting came to an end, there were off-the-cuff remarks inferring I would be passed over for promotion.

(A) Delete *over*

(B) Replace the comma with a semicolon

(C) Replace *inferring* with *implying*

(D) Delete the hyphen in *closed-door*

(144)   Select the action that correctly modifies the following statement:

After going through both copies, the English professor concluded that the rough draft was the best copy.

(A) Correct the misplaced modifier

(B) Replace *best* with *better*

(C) Lowercase *English*

(D) Insert quotation marks on *rough* to imply irony

(145)   Which region in China has the largest population?

(A) Southern region of China

(B) Western region of China

(C) Northern region of China

(D) Eastern region of China

(146)   In which world region is Latin America located?

(A) South America, excluding Brazil

(B) To the south of United States in the Western Hemisphere

(C) Mexico, Guatemala and Belize

(D) South America

(147)   Name the geographic feature with the largest impact on Polish history.

(A) The location of the Great European Plain

(B) Many rivers

(C) Impassable mountains

(D) Very cold winters

(148)   When is a country said to be doubly landlocked?

(A) When it lacks access to the sea and does not have rivers

(B) When it is not only landlocked but also lacks main airports

(C) When it lacks access to the sea

(D) When that country and its neighbors are all landlocked

(149)   A topological map can best be used for:

(A) Recognizing Kansas's main crops

(B) Identifying the city's population

(C) Counting the number of states in the United States

(D) Identifying mountain height

(150)   What has been the result of the Sahara Desert on Africa's development?

(A) It promoted the invention of other energy strategies

(B) It promoted agriculture around Africa

(C) It led to separate development of the northern regions of Africa and sub-Saharan Africa

(D) It has inhibited Africa's development

(151)   Why are the Suez Canal and the Strait of Gibraltar important?

(A) They are appropriate strategic points for launching attacks

(B) They facilitate the Mediterranean trade

(C) They are the two man-made water routes in the Mediterranean region

(D) The two waterways were initially under British control

(152)   Why did Russia try to conquer Turkey in the 1800s?

(A) Turkey acts as an entry point into the Middle East

(B) Russia hoped access to Europe would grant it leverage

(C) Russia wanted to strategically secure itself in the event that it was attacked

(D) Russia wanted a warm-water port

(153)   Name the geographical feature that played a major role in China's development.

(A) The north and west mountain ranges

(B) Frequent earthquakes

(C) No coastline ports

(D) No major rivers

(154)   Name the geographic element that was a contributing factor to isolationism in America.

(A) The oceans located in the west and east

(B) The Appalachians and the Rockies

(C) The north's bitterly cold weather

(D) The deserts located in the southwest

(155) In which period were modern European towns developed?

(A) The Roman Era

(B) The Middle Ages

(C) After World War I

(D) During the Renaissance

(156) What was the most notable long-term effect of the Crusades?

(A) The demise of European knights

(B) The demand of goods from the East

(C) The growth of Islam in Europe

(D) The destruction of Ottoman society

(157) What element contributed to the flourishing of the Renaissance in the northern part of Italy?

(A) Loyalty to the Byzantine Church

(B) The existence of democratic city-states

(C) Free expression brought about by liberal laws

(D) The wealthy elite that supported artwork

(158) Select the ethical system that is closely parallel to Bushido, the code of conduct that the Japanese samurai adhered to.

(A) Buddhist pacifism

(B) Medieval chivalry

(C) Enlightenment-era humanism

(D) The Ten Commandments

(159) Which of the following is vital for industrialization?

(A) Food surplus

(B) Democratic government

(C) Universal education

(D) Protection of human rights

(160) What was the social category that obtained great power in 1789 following the French Revolution?

(A) The royal family

(B) The military

(C) The Catholic Church

(D) The middle class

(161)   Which of the following resulted from Stalin's agricultural collectivization program?

(A) Shift from producing costly foods to producing staple foods

(B) Food shortages

(C) The growing reliance on the fishing industry

(D) Food surpluses

(162)   Which of the following did not at all contribute to the development of WWI?

(A) Religious violence

(B) Increased nationalism

(C) Increased militarism

(D) A complex web of alliances

(163)   Which event compelled the emperor of Japan to describe himself as "only human?"

(A) The bombing of Hiroshima

(B) The opening of Japan

(C) The bombing of Pearl Harbor

(D) The loss of World War II

(164) What novel provision did the United States insist be part of the new Japanese constitution after World War II?

(A) A reduction in Japanese military size

(B) The free trade treaty with the United States

(C) A section banning the practice of Shinto by Japanese lawmakers

(D) Accepting a permanent US military base in Okinawa

(165) What characteristic was common in both the Soviet Union and Nazi Germany before World War II?

(A) One-party government in control

(B) Independent media

(C) Command property

(D) The protection of property rights

(166) What was Gorbachev's policy in the 1980s?

(A) Collectivization

(B) Bolshevism

(C) Glasnost

(D) Collectivization

(167) Which nation does not regard itself as communist?

(A) Vietnam

(B) North Korea

(C) Cuba

(D) Laos

(168) Which of the following happened next after the Roman Empire fell?

(A) Royal families balancing power

(B) Organized city-states decentralizing their power

(C) The emergence of democratic nations

(D) Weak central government and general mayhem

(169) In which city did Aristotle, Socrates and Plato teach philosophy?

(A) Rome

(B) Sparta

(C) Athens

(D) Cairo

(170) Name the nation that was once ruled by the Mamluks, Fatimids and Ayyubids.

(A) Kuwait

(B) Egypt

(C) Syria

(D) Lebanon

(171)   What differentiates Andalusia from the rest of Spain?

(A) It was ruled under Islamic law for about 700 years

(B) The citizens followed the Byzantine Church

(C) Its flat landscape was different from the mountainous north

(D) It was often attacked by Norse invaders

(172)   Name the first European to locate North America.

(A) Ferdinand Magellan

(B) Leif Ericson

(C) Amerigo Vespucci

(D) Christopher Columbus

(173)   What was the primary goal of the African National Congress during apartheid?

(A) Establish the one-person one-vote system

(B) Free Nelson Mandela

(C) Create a federal state granting each race its own homeland

(D) Drive Afrikaners out of South Africa

(174)   What factor do Kemal Ataturk and Gamal Nasser have in common?

(A) They both attempted to secularize their nations

(B) They both tried to modernize their nations

(C) They both consolidated control by establishing a one-party political rule

(D) Neither had a strong relationship with the West

(175) According to the US Constitution, which government branch is supreme?

(A) Judiciary

(B) Executive

(C) Legislature

(D) None

(176) George Washington was a member of the _____ political party.

(A) Whig

(B) Republican

(C) Democrat

(D) He was not in any political party.

(177) What is the function of the Department of the Interior?

(A) Maintenance of US government buildings

(B) Management of US natural resources and heritage sites

(C) Coordination of internal transportation

(D) Protection of US internal security

(178) What is the department assigned to manage US borders?

(A) Department of the Interior

(B) Department of Defense

(C) Department of Homeland Security

(D) Department of State

(179) What is the US military branch that does not report back to the secretary of Defense?

(A) The Marines

(B) All branches

(C) The Coast Guard

(D) The army

(180) The top rank in the US Army is:

(A) General of Armies

(B) Secretary General

(C) Chairman of the Joint Chief of Staff

(D) General of the Army

(181) What one factor does not guarantee US citizenship?

(A) Going through the nationalization process

(B) Having one parent who is a US citizen

(C) Being born in Puerto Rico

(D) Being born in the United States

(182) Massachusetts, Virginia, Kentucky and Pennsylvania are all commonwealth states. What is their legal difference from the other 46 states?

(A) There is no legal difference

(B) They have larger local sovereignty

(C) The legal differences that once existed have been overruled by federal law

(D) Their legislatures are organized differently

(183) What organization does not belong to the US government?

(A) The Securities Exchange Commission

(B) The World Bank

(C) The Peace Corps

(D) The Smithsonian Institute

(184) What is a controversial method used by a president to dismiss a bill without directly vetoing it?

(A) Tabling

(B) Pocket veto

(C) Filibuster

(D) Cloture

(185)   A blueprint has a line whose length is 1.5 yards. In the blueprint, 1 yard represents 0.9 meters. Roughly how long is that line in terms of meters?

(A) 2.4 meters

(B) 1.35 meters

(C) 0.6 meters

(D) 1.67 meters

(186)   Snacks sold in Country X last year raised revenue totaling $12 billion, made up of 34% from potato chips, 17% from tortilla chips, 13% from nuts, 13% from popcorn, 12% from pretzels and 11% from other snacks. From this information, calculate the ratio of potato chip revenue to tortilla chip revenue.

(A) 2:1

(B) 1:2

(C) 3:2

(D) 2:3

(187)   Snacks sold in Country X last year raised revenue totaling $12 billion, made up of 34% from potato chips, 17% from tortilla chips, 13% from nuts, 13% from popcorn, 12% from pretzels and 11% from other snacks. Thirty percent of the revenue received from the sale of potato chips specifically came from the sale of barbeque potato chips. This means the amount of revenue that came from the sale of barbeque potato chips was:

(A) $1.2 billion

(B) $2.4 billion

(C) $3.6 billion

(D) $0.6 billion

(188) Lauren's earnings are $8.40 every hour, and the rate of overtime equals one and a half times the regular hourly rate. Overtime is any time Lauren exceeds 40 hours of work. If she works 45 hours in a week, what should her total pay be?

(A) $567

(B) $336

(C) $399

(D) $370

(189) Jane's shadow is 5 feet long while her father's shadow is 8 feet long. Jane's father is 6 feet tall. What is Jane's height?

(A) 4 ft 6 in

(B) 6 ft 8 in

(C) 4 ft 10 in

(D) 3 ft 9 in

(190) Amit donates 4/13ths of his January paycheck to charity. In absolute figures, the amount he donates is $26.80. Calculate Amit's January paycheck in full.

(A) $348.40

(B) $8.25

(C) $87.10

(D) $82.50

(191)   Given that x = 2, calculate x + x(xx)

(A) 10

(B) 64

(C) 18

(D) 36

(192) Mr. Kamau sold two pipes, each at $1.20. From one pipe he made a profit of 20% based on the cost of the pipe, whereas from the other he made a loss of 20%, also based on the cost of the pipe. From this information, choose the answer option that is correct.

(A) Overall, Mr. Kamau broke even

(B) Overall, Mr. Kamau lost 4 cents

(C) Overall, Mr. Kamau gained 10 cents

(D) Overall, Mr. Kamau lost 10 cents

(193) Jacques arrived in Paris by flight from Tokyo and exchanged his 50,000 yen for the equivalent francs (F). Considering a single US dollar was equivalent to 140 yen and was also equivalent to 6 francs, what is roughly the amount of francs that Jacques received?

(A) 1,167 F

(B) 4,200 F

(C) 2,143 F

(D) 63 F

(194) If the rate at which Tom's savings account earns interest is 2 1/4% annually, what is the amount of interest he is expected to have earned by the end of the fifth consecutive year if he maintains a deposit of $1,000?

(A) $150

(B) $22.50

(C) $112.50

(D) $100

(195) Which of the following is not required for a perfect market?

(A) Equal access to technology

(B) No barriers in market entry and exit

(C) Every market player having total access to all information pertaining to the market

(D) No regulation

(196) Which of the following does not exemplify insider trading?

(A) Someone within the organization makes use of confidential information to do business

(B) Someone within a partner organization makes use of confidential information to do business

(C) Someone receives information in confidence from a close friend who works in a company and utilizes that information to do business

(D) Someone reads information about the organization from a newspaper and does business with the organization the same week

(197)   If a company has full control of its product's life cycle from the beginning of production or sourcing of raw materials to selling the product, the term used is:

(A) Vertical integration

(B) Monopoly

(C) Economies of scale

(D) Horizontal integration

(198)   All of the activities listed below are legal in the United States apart from:

(A) Economies of scale

(B) Vertical integration

(C) Activities of a monopolistic nature

(D) Horizontal integration

(199)   Which of the economic systems listed below is run with an underlying assumption that a nation's wealth is dependent on the country's total capital?

(A) Feudalism

(B) Capitalism

(C) Bullionism

(D) Mercantilism

(200) What is arbitrage?

(A) Earning profits when you manipulate a discrepancy in different markets

(B) A particular system with the capacity to make large legal trades

(C) Trading in stocks via intermediaries

(D) An arbitration system for trading disputes

Test 2: Answers & Explanations

(1) What major role does the board of directors play?

The correct answer is: (A) Representing the shareholders

The main role the board of directors plays is representing the shareholders, who are essentially the company owners. It is the responsibility of the board to act in the interest of the shareholders. Incidentally, board members can also be shareholders, although their size of shares should be disclosed and no board members should own shares beyond a certain percentage allowed by company policy.

(2) Which of the statements listed below explains what differentiates a vision statement from a mission statement?

The correct answer is: (C) The guidelines provided by the mission statement are more pragmatic than those the vision statement provides

The major difference between a mission statement and a vision statement is the guidelines each of them contains. While the mission statement's guidelines are pragmatic, those of the vision statement are less so. From the vision statement you can see only the company's grand plan and general direction, but from the mission statement you see how the plans will be implemented.

(3) If a grocery store franchise decides to buy out several farms in your locality and starts farming so it can grow its own supplies, the strategy this franchise will have implemented is referred to as:

The correct answer is: (B) Backward integration

Backward integration is used to describe a situation in which a company expands its activities by taking up tasks that were previously done by other businesses up its supply chain. Backward integration is a kind of vertical integration. In vertical integration, a firm takes over two or more functions previously performed by different businesses.

One common means companies use to implement backward integration is acquiring or merging with the businesses carrying out the tasks they would like to take up. At the end of the day, the company implementing backward integration ends up saving on cost of production or doing business by taking up several supply chain levels and incorporating them into one production line.

The reason the process is termed "backward" is that the company in question takes one step behind the normal supply chain and integrates the tasks into its main business.

(4) Which of the options below does not automatically lead to increased competition among companies?

The correct answer is: (D) Industry deregulation

Whether competition increases or not is dependent on the particular government regulations being scrapped.

When there are many competitors in a given industry, companies strategize about ways to take one another's clients, thus increasing competition. The same case applies when growth in the industry is slow. As for increased overheads, they make it necessary for companies to up their game and become more competitive just to survive in an environment where cost of production and business in general keep rising with every increment in cost of overheads. This is the reason option (D) is the most appropriate answer.

(5) Which of the business strategies listed below depends on production that has to be adjusted in order to satisfy immediate demand in the market and bring down costs linked to idle time for employees and facilities?

The correct answer is: (B) Production done on a just-in-time basis

The correct strategy is (B), where production is done on a just-in-time (JIT) basis. This is a strategy used in the manufacturing sector. Sometimes it is also referred to as the "Toyota Production System" (TPS). Its main aim is to reduce time spent in the process of production and also the time taken to respond to an issue raised by suppliers and customers.

For the production system to consume the minimum amount of time possible, the processes employed must be dependable. This dependability then leads to a reduction of overhead costs. Ultimately the company enjoys a competitive advantage.

(6) Which of the options listed below does not exemplify a strong infrastructure that provides a competitive advantage?

The correct answer is: (D) The marketing department helping the company penetrate an entirely new market

Even if the marketing department helps the company penetrate a market that is entirely new, this does not exemplify a strong infrastructure that gives the company any competitive advantage. It does not put the company ahead of other competing companies in any tangible way.

What constitutes a strong infrastructure is the enabling of activities like those of a legal nature in the company, management and quality assurance, purchasing and matters of a financial nature. The term "competitive advantage" is used for whatever strategic advantage there may be in a firm to make it more competitive than its rivals. A firm with a competitive advantage is likely to have good relationships with various regulators in the industry and its customers and to have more efficient IT systems than its rivals.

(7) One way you can tell when a company is able to meet its short-term obligations is:

The correct answer is: (A) Its level of liquidity

You can tell how liquid a company is if it is in a position to fulfill its short-term financial obligations. The ratio of total short-term assets that include cash in hand and short-term debtors compared to short-term debts like loan interest and wages shows a company's level of liquidity.

The debts included in the short-term assets are only those expected to be repaid within a few months' time, which must also not be doubtful. Doubtful debts are those owed by people who do not have a good credit record. These are individuals who are likely to fail to repay their debts in time.

Sometimes a profitable company may not have sufficient assets that can be quickly converted into cash, and such companies sometimes take out cheap loans to meet their short-term financial obligations.

(8) One reason a software company might have a market value that's larger than its book value is:

The correct answer is: (A) The market includes the company's intellectual property in its overall value

The reason the company's market value might be higher than its book value is that the company's intellectual properties or assets also have value, yet such assets are not included in the books when the company is starting out. Part of this could be goodwill, considering potential clients can easily trust the capacity of the company's software engineers to come up with a competitive program even without looking at the firm's balance sheet.

(9) In order for a company to alleviate high turnover of staff within a competitive industry, the company should:

The correct answer is: (D) Introduce programs geared toward retaining employees

Programs meant for employee-retention efforts are great in a situation in which there is a threat of staff leaving en masse or in a manner that will destabilize operations or increase recruitment costs. The term "staff retention" is used for the degree or level to which existing employees stay with their employer over a specified period of time.

Often the employee-retention programs companies put in place target various needs employees seem to have, in particular those affecting their level of job satisfaction. Such retention programs are meant to discourage existing staff from leaving the firm and instead be excited to stay. It is advisable for a firm to implement programs geared toward raising the level of staff retention because increased staff turnover causes difficulties when it comes to implementing serious company strategies.

This is because teams involved are often weak because of constantly having new staff members who do not necessarily work well with other team members. Among the incentives a company can include in an employee-retention program are better health benefits; perks offered at the workplace, such as company-sponsored lunches and gym facilities; attractive retirement plans; and opportunities to take up company stock options.

(10) Who is involved in employee evaluation during a 360° evaluation process?

The correct answer is: (D) Subordinates, colleagues and managers

When it comes to the 360° process of evaluation, subordinates, colleagues and managers are all involved in providing feedback. Sometimes feedback is also sought from customers. The aim of using this method is to get a comprehensive picture of a person's skills from the perspective of all the people who interact with that person in the workplace.

(11) During the past decade or so, modern IT systems have had significant impact on some aspects of business. Choose one aspect below that has been most impacted.

The correct answer is: (C) Increase in social capital

Social capital has to do with enhancing interpersonal relationships through networks, something that makes people work together more efficiently. Modern IT systems have made such interactions easier, and now coworkers are able to interact more conveniently without wasting a lot of company time. Email is one example of a tool that has improved social capital.

Social interactions have also been enhanced through social media, where colleagues are also able to share issues of personal interest. These IT systems have, therefore, enhanced understanding among employees, and often this makes them able to cooperate better as they use the different platforms to enhance their shared values. In short, it has become increasingly important for people to build social networks, and this in turn builds social capital.

(12) Which of the qualities listed below is not a good leadership characteristic?

The correct answer is: (D) Being reactive

People who are reactive are prompted to act by something that has happened, so they are simply responding to an outcome. On the other hand, people who are proactive act of their own accord at their own chosen time. Proactive people are good at planning, and such planning charts the way forward in a deliberate manner. When people are reactive sometimes they panic, and in the process they can make others panic as well. In such circumstances it becomes difficult for people to bring things back under control.

Being reactive is not a good trait for a leader. It precludes any possibility of thinking ahead and planning, and so such a leader hardly has any strategy that can be effectively implemented.

(13) Which of the answers listed below details a failure that is common in businesses that are barely able to keep up with their daily functions?

The correct answer is: (D) Each of the failures listed above

When a company can barely keep up with its day-to-day tasks, it has failed to carry out an analysis of its operations in an objective manner. It also has not been evaluating its strategic objectives or aims. It is likely the company is taking some actions on the basis of wrong assumptions, hence the inability to get good results in the prevailing business environment.

It is advisable to periodically take time to look at what is happening in the business, to assess the daily tasks being undertaken and observe the bigger picture to see how they fit in. Looking at the overall business picture allows companies to make adjustments when they realize they are not moving in the right direction.

(14) Which of the activities listed below is not a management technique referred to as "management by walking around"?

The correct answer is: (B) Having set questions for particular people to respond to

When you manage your staff or business by walking around (known as MBWA), it means you are assessing the business premises in a casual manner, so that whoever wants to point out something to you will, and whoever does not will just continue working.

This provides an opportunity for an employee to open up in a safe environment, as opposed to addressing a manager in his or her office, which can be intimidating. Consequently, employees trust you more, and soon you are able to casually ask questions about how they are doing; questions that they respond to with ease while opening up about issues that may be affecting the company, sometimes negatively.

In such circumstances you get a chance to seek employees' opinion regarding the best way to solve the problem they have observed. MBWA requires you to keep an open mind at all times and to avoid interrogating employees as you walk around.

(15) The relationship that should exist between a corporate structure and strategy is:

The correct answer is: (A) Corporate structure designed to enable implementation of the corporate strategy

The term "corporate structure" is used for the way a company's departments are organized, or how the different units comprising the business are organized. Different companies can have structures that vary, and that usually depends on the industry the company is operating in. As for corporate strategy, it is the major plan the company develops regarding how to pick its market and develop it to beat the competition while enhancing operations in its internal business divisions.

Any time a corporate structure is being formed, the aim should be to enable implementation of the corporate strategy. Certainly, there must be some cost incurred when you want to reorganize the company, but it helps to have a corporate strategy created to be effective from the start.

(16) What is one of the advantages associated with the corporate structure of a holding company?

The correct answer is: (A) Reduction of overhead costs and those related to personnel, enabled by the small size of the corporation's office

A holding company is able to keep its overhead and personnel costs at a minimum because it runs a relatively small office. The corporate office structure is suitable only when the decision-making process is decentralized. For example, a corporate office structure is desirable when there is a single management company that is the owner of different companies operating in various industries.

You may have, for example, a holding company that owns both a chain of international hotels and a big real estate firm. In such a case, the holding company needs only a small office, probably with fewer than five employees, because it does not run the day-to-day operations of either the hotel chain or the real estate business. This means the cost of electricity, water and other utilities plus the wage bill and other employee benefits will be very small compared to other companies.

(17) What is one of the risks of outsourcing?

The correct answer is: (B) Loss of critical skills

The term "outsourcing" is used for the practice within the business world of hiring an entity outside the company and entrusting them with delivery of services that would otherwise have been done by staff within the company. It can also entail production of goods that are normally produced by the company employees at the normal place of business. Outsourcing is very popular with companies trying to cut costs and downsize by reducing the number of employees. One risk that comes with outsourcing is losing experienced employees when their jobs become redundant. Assuming that the worst happens and the company outsourced to goes under, the company that did the outsourcing is then left scrambling, without a capable workforce. For that reason, the decision to outsource should be made only after careful evaluation of both the company's situation and the company that may be outsourced to.

(18) When a company is faced with a challenging business environment, the best way to proceed is:

The correct answer is: (D) Innovate controls for strategic purposes, which are suitable for the prevailing environment

A company struggling in the prevailing business environment must innovate and create strategic controls that suit the prevailing environment. Making detailed plans is not often helpful under the circumstances, although it is important for everyone involved to seek a solution to understand clearly what is at stake, or what exactly the company needs to achieve. The company should set milestones that are clear to all involved, because these help determine the progress being made and the pace at which it is being achieved.

(19) Which of these things is not associated with setting short-term goals?

The correct answer is: (B) Emphasizing best performance

Emphasizing best performance is a positive asset in a business, but it does not constitute effective setting of short-term goals. If you set goals that are not well defined, there are bound to be instances of ambiguity as work progresses, and there is a great likelihood you will need to adjust the expectations along the way. Once this happens, the purpose of setting the original short-term goals is defeated.

(20)   Emphasizing corporate culture and offering intangible rewards becomes very useful when:

The correct answer is: (A) The work being performed is of a creative nature and requires self-direction

When the work requires a creative, self-directed employee, corporate culture comes in handy and offering intangible rewards serves as great motivation. Even for any manager who might wish to institute regulations, it may not be clear what the best way is to design such rules and make them effective. The reality is that if you introduce rules that are poorly crafted, they could end up impeding productivity.

(21) One major difference between a joint venture and a strategic alliance is that:

The correct answer is: (C) In a joint venture, a third-party entity must be created

While it is necessary to create a third party when entering into a joint venture, this is not necessary when engaging in a strategic alliance. A joint venture is carried out by a newly formed company whose participants are owners of different companies. Often a joint venture is started with a particular business function or task in mind; once it is accomplished, the life of the joint venture comes to an end.

The term "joint venture" is used to describe a business arrangement between two parties or more pooling resources in a bid to accomplish a particular mutual goal. The task could constitute an entire project or an independent activity of a business nature.

(22)   It is reasonable for stockholders to expect company managers to:

The correct answer is: (A) Make their investment more valuable

At all times, company managers should bear in mind the objective of increasing the value of stockholders' investment. Such increases indicate the company is growing and has a bright future.

The issue of managing the stockholders' portfolio does not fall under the responsibilities of company managers. All stockholders, as investors, are responsible for managing their portfolio, and they have a choice to hire an expert to advise them accordingly.

(23)   A company should consider undertaking vertical integration when:

The correct answer is: (A) It is important to reduce the costs of transacting and improve coordination

When it is important to reduce the costs of transacting and improve coordination, it is advisable for a company to undertake vertical integration. Remember, when a company understands vertical integration, it is able to take on a bigger part of the value chain. Good examples of vertical integration are forward integration and backward integration.

(24)   When you have a company's head office continuously advising its subsidiaries, this is referred to as:

The correct answer is: (B) Parenting

A company that keeps monitoring the operations of its subsidiaries while closely advising them is said to be engaged in parenting. This term should not be taken in a negative sense, because it simply describes the company's willingness to mentor those subsidiaries so that they flourish.

Not all parent companies behave the same toward their subsidiaries where monitoring is concerned. When the parent company is hands-on, its subsidiaries are unlikely to fold in the first few years of business, as the parent company is able to identify challenges that are potentially damaging and advise the subsidiary on how to handle them.

(25)   Among the options listed below, which represents a strategic alliance that is not wise for a business?

The correct answer is: (D) Relying on documents for governing to ensure the smooth running of the venture

Relying on documents when trying to ensure smooth and effective running of a venture is not wise if you are in a strategic alliance. It is better for the partners to work mutually and cohesively among themselves than to insist on following documented protocols. All the parties involved should be made to feel they are acting voluntarily and in good faith, and are trusted by everyone else involved.

(26)   Every company hopes to be in a position to earn beyond normal profits. What is the meaning of "normal profits"?

The correct answer is: (B) A return that enables a business to cover risk and remain in business

If what the business earns over a specified period is sufficient to cover its cost of earning that amount and still have enough to keep it running normally, then the return it attains is referred to as normal profit. In order for a business to stay competitive in its industry, it is important that it generate enough revenue to cover the costs it incurs during its daily operations. It is also important that the business have extra income to help in carrying out the necessary daily tasks.

Investors use normal profits to compare a business' performance against others that incur similar risk. If a business is found to have great returns compared to its level of risk, investors want to have it in their portfolio.

(27)   One of the required factors for a market to be deemed mature is:

The correct answer is: (A) Low rate of growth and high intensity of competition

When a business has ceased to grow, yet the field remains very competitive, it is a sign that business has reached maturity. In order to reduce operating costs, such a business needs to pay more attention to its processes with a view to making them more efficient. Of course, it needs to continue maintaining the quality and general competitiveness of its products.

(28)   The literacy rate in the United States was greatly impacted by a change instituted at the national level in the 1800s. What change was it?

The correct answer is: (A) Making education compulsory

Making education compulsory contributed immensely to raising the level of literacy in the United States. Education was made compulsory a short time before the beginning of the Civil War, starting in Massachusetts in 1852. The same state had passed similar legislation in 1647. That 1852 legislation required all cities and towns to establish a primary school where the focus would be on grammar and basic arithmetic. Owing to that effort to have people educated, a good number of soldiers were able to communicate through letters during the Civil War.

(29)   What significant role do syndicates in the news industry play?

The correct answer is: (C) They gather and sell work compiled by journalists and photographers as well as other contributors en masse

Syndicates play the role of gathering and selling journalists' work en masse, and they do the same with work compiled by photographers as well as other participants within the news industry. For example, stories that have been written specifically for the Associated Press or Reuters also appear in other newspapers across the globe.

(30)   In the late 1800s, magazines reduced their prices in a drastic way. What caused that big drop in magazine prices?

The correct answer is: (B) A rise in revenues from advertising

Since magazine printers could cover some of their costs through the revenues received from advertising, they were able to lower the prices of magazines and still continue in business without encountering financial problems.

Advertising became popular in the 1800s, and it was mostly done through newspapers and magazines. Such publications were released on a weekly basis, and so people could anticipate advertisements with the same regularity. Many publications were used to advertise books and various other materials for reading. What made advertising even more lucrative is the fact that from 1850 to the1860s, middle-class people were excited about reading the advertisements that promoted various products, especially those newly released into the market. Printed publications became their go-to material.

(31) Muckraking is:

The correct answer is: (C) Provoking particular individuals or groups of people so they take action

Often, muckraking targets people who are powerful in government or in society, and politicians are good examples. The people involved in muckraking, generally referred to as muckrakers, focus on the anger their reporting is bound to arouse in people, hoping it will be sufficient to make them demand more change that will improve their welfare.

(32) The first time radio was used as a major medium for dissemination of news was:

The correct answer is: (A) In WWII

During WWII, radio was extensively used to disseminate news. This trend continued for decades, until the television was invented and people began to rely on it more for news. In fact, many people in the United States—around 60% of households—bought radios between 1923 and 1930.

As for TVs, they were embraced by Americans in the 1940s, and half of US families had a black-and-white television set by 1955.

(33) What is meant by a "pseudo-event"?

The correct answer is: (B) An event designed specifically to garner publicity

When you organize an event and its major purpose is to gain publicity, such an event is said to be a pseudo-event. "Pseudo" means "not genuine," so a pseudo-event is not a real event like others with a substantial purpose. A PR event cannot be termed a pseudo-event, as it has a genuine purpose of raising awareness, among other things. On the contrary, a pseudo-event is stage-managed.

(34)   The 1938 Foreign Agents Registration Act's target was Ivy Lee, a pioneer in public relations. What did he do to prompt the enactment of that law?

The correct answer is: (C) Represented Germany during the Nazi regime

The 1938 Foreign Agents Registration Act was enacted because Ivy Lee agreed to represent Germany during the Nazi regime. The law was designed to apply to anyone who agrees to represent the interests of any government other than the US government. According to the legislation, such an agent is required to disclose the existing relationship with the foreign power and explain exactly what the involvement is in terms of activities and financial matters.

(35)   When professionals in public relations (PR) perform their work, their target audiences are:

The correct answer is (D) Employees, shareholders and the public in general

The aim of engaging a PR firm is to help manage reputation. With regards to government, PR means managing the government's reputation in the eyes of everyone, both domestic and local.

A PR department disseminates the correct information about a firm. The target consumers of the information include the employees themselves, the company, the shareholders and anyone else who might find the information helpful. Often this department creates different versions of documents for a wide range of audiences.

(36)   The function of public affairs differs from that of public relations in that:

The correct answer is: (C) The professionals in public affairs work with influential institutions on behalf of their company

The function of public affairs is a subset of public relations. The professionals in public affairs are charged with dealing with regulatory bodies and politicians as well as other influential groups, always on the company's behalf. Overall, public affairs efforts are geared toward establishing and developing good relationships between powerful institutions and groups and a company or government. At the end of the day, the public affairs function ends up enhancing public relations.

The work that professionals in public affairs do includes government relations and media communication; management of diverse issues; corporate and social responsibility, often abbreviated as CSR; dissemination of information; and strategic communication. Great PR can be effective in influencing public policy, building and maintaining a strong reputation and finding mutual ground with stakeholders.

(37)   The standard unit used to express the efficiency of a given advertisement is:

The correct answer is: (B) Cost per thousand

Cost per thousand is the standard unit used to express the efficiency of a given advertisement. In short, how much does a given advertisement attract readership? Note that in cases in which a magazine already has a large readership, it can still charge a significant amount of money for advertisements and still have a low CPT.

(38)   What is the correct meaning of a paradigm?

The correct answer is: (B) A particular theory responsible for organizing information pertaining to the world

Simply put, a paradigm helps organize information pertaining to the world. It does not mean that a given paradigm is always accurate. But even with its inaccuracies, it can still be helpful as long as you acknowledge its shortcomings.

A paradigm is a perspective or way to look at something. In the business arena, this term could be used to point to an approach used to reach customers or succeed in revenue creation. A paradigm is closely linked to communication, and philosopher Thomas Kuhn saw it as a wide framework guiding the way scholars think and conduct their research into specific theories over a long period of time.

In matters associated with the Foreign Service, a paradigm shift can lead to change in foreign policy.

(39)   The mass communication theory of two-step flow can be summarized as:

The correct answer is: (A) Ideas keep flowing from makers of opinions to followers of opinions

This theory that the flow of ideas begins with opinion makers and moves to reach opinion followers is significant because it guides you when you want to influence thinking in one way or another. The theory is that if you influence opinion makers, you will also indirectly influence everyone else.

(40)   Klapper's reinforcement theory of mass media is that:

The correct answer is: (C) The power it has can reinforce only beliefs that already exist

According to Klapper's reinforcement theory, mass media has power that can reinforce only existing beliefs. People consuming information from the media often choose to take seriously only the media that concurs with their beliefs.

(41) Which of the options below exemplifies setting an agenda?

The correct answer is: (A) An editor chooses to print on the first page of the newspaper a story that can politically embarrass someone

When a newspaper editor chooses to run a on the paper's front page story that can politically embarrass someone, the purpose is to set an agenda, such as discrediting a particular politician. That decision may also be intended to promote a different politician, as readers are likely to make comparisons between the politician being discredited and his or her rivals.

The people who support this role of the media assert that the media is not interested in telling people the way they should think, but instead it is interested in giving them material to weigh. Whatever the true intention of the media is, the fact is that this manner of guiding conversation is powerful.

(42)   What is the theory that holds that media creates an image that is accepted only because people make a choice to believe that image?

The correct answer is: (D) Cultivation theory

The people who support this theory believe that it is possible for media to shape audiences' view of the world even if information is presented incorrectly.

The theory posits that when people spend a lot of time watching media like TV, they end up believing that what is presented in the media is the social reality, whereas that may not be the case.

(43)   Companies that deal with polling normally seek public opinion using:

The correct answer is: (A) Sampling

Polling organizations use the sampling method to estimate public opinion. If the particular sample used provides answers that are reflective of the larger population's opinion, then that particular poll can be said to be accurate.

Sampling is favored by polling companies because it can be done at minimal cost as opposed to other methods, such as a census. Samples are also much smaller than an entire population, and polling by use of sampling proves to be much faster and more accurate.

(44)   Modern-day presidential campaigns tend to put their focus primarily on _____ because of being influenced by the media.

The correct answer is: (B) The varying personalities of the candidates

In modern day US presidential campaigns, a lot of emphasis is put on the personality of each candidate because that is what the media is mostly interested in. Journalists want to keep the audience interested, so they create narratives geared toward maintaining an audience's interest. Hence the media leads people to interpret events largely on the basis of the candidates' respective public personas as opposed to the agendas the candidates are running on.

(45)   Which of the options below provides an accurate description of libel?

The correct answer is: (A) Reporting that is false and malicious and causes damage to a person's reputation

To qualify as libelous, the reporting must be published, false and malicious, and it also must be seen to be damaging to a person's reputation. Another way to describe libel is defamation that is in written form.

There is no protection against libel in the First Amendment so option (C) cannot be correct. There are some countries where you can be sued for libel even when the information reported is accurate; the big determinant is whether the information is damaging to a person's reputation.

(46)   Sometimes the question of whether or not a source of information should be shielded arises. Is it the right of a journalist to shield or protect a source of confidential information?

The correct answer is: (B) That depends on which US state the issue has arisen in

Journalists' rights to shield their sources depend on the particular state the matter arises in. Different states regulate journalists' rights differently from others, and there is no federal law pertaining to protection of confidential sources by journalists. However, the Supreme Court has acknowledged journalists have some protection under the First Amendment, while at the same time noting they are not immune to grand jury subpoenas.

(47)   Which country spearheaded the initiation of Radio Free Europe?

The correct answer is: (D) The United States

In 1949 the United States created and funded what is today referred to as Radio Liberty, but which at the beginning was referred to as Radio Free Europe. In its early days, it was meant to be used for propaganda against communism. Today, Radio Free Europe seeks to transmit news and different analyses to different nations whose local media faces censorship.

Many of the countries targeted are in Eastern Europe and Central Asia, as well as the Middle East. The radio broadcast is supervised just like other US broadcasting services by the US Agency for Global Media.

(48)   Whenever someone close to you nods in the middle of a conversation as you speak, it exemplifies:

The correct answer is: (A) Providing feedback during personal communication

When someone nods to you as you are engaged in private conversation, especially someone you refer to as a friend, this is a way for that person to give you feedback regarding what you have just said. This form of feedback happens so naturally that the person providing it is hardly conscious of it. During such communication, people keep giving one another subtle cues to guide the conversation's direction.

(49)   There is a well-known statement Marshall McLuhan made, which is, "The medium is the message." The meaning of this statement is that:

The correct answer is: (B) People are more concerned about the medium being used than the particular content being delivered

Marshall McLuhan argued that when a person becomes a prolific reader, such a person is not attached to any particular book, but instead just wants any material or book to read. In McLuhan's view, the theory of communication should be about studying different types of communication media as opposed to the specific content communicated.

(50)   Which of the options below exemplifies technological determinism?

The correct answer is: (C) Believing that society will break down specifically because of the internet

Technological determinism assumes the internet and advancements in technology in general will be responsible for the breakdown of society.

(51) The very first form of media to be mass-produced was:

The correct answer is: (A) Books

Books led in mass media production. Using the printing press invented by Johannes Gutenberg, people could create their own books en masse, then sell them at low prices. The printing press Gutenberg created was movable, and it is credited with revolutionizing how knowledge was transmitted.

Although Gutenberg began to experiment with printing in 1440 when living in France, it was not until he went back to Mainz, Germany, that he perfected his skills. He developed his printing machine in 1450. The technology of Gutenberg's printing machine become revolutionary, especially because of the way it enabled information to be disseminated across Europe during the 15th century.

(52) Which of the options below best defines "literacy"?

The correct answer is: (B) The capacity to make use of a particular medium

Literacy is the capacity one has to effectively use a particular medium as is explained in option (B). However, although "literacy" is a term usually used to refer to language in written form, it can also be used to refer to different media. For example, having the capacity to make use of the internet qualifies you to say you have some level of computer literacy.

(53) How can "genre" best be defined?

The correct answer is: (C) Grouped works in a particular medium, sharing several conventions

The best way to define "genre" is as grouped work in a particular medium that shares a number of conventions. For example if you have a number of novels and notice some of them have swords and sorcery in them, you can reasonably assume that you are reading novels in the fantasy genre.

(54) The voting trend or behavior people adopt is mostly influenced by:

The correct answer is: (D) Conversations they have with their friends

Although the other options listed—print media, television and online media—also have some impact on the way people vote, the greatest influence or effect comes from conversations people share as friends. Many people say they get a lot of political information through online media, but at the end of the day, friends' opinions have been shown to matter to people and mostly end up influencing the way they vote.

(55) What is meant by the "CNN effect"?

The correct answer is: (A) The power televised media has in setting the agenda

The term "CNN effect" was coined by Madeleine Albright, who served as US Secretary of State from 1997 to 2001 when President Clinton was in office. The very first woman to hold that position in the United States, she immigrated to the United States from Czechoslovakia in 1948.

In coining the term "CNN effect," Albright observed the manner in which CNN influenced decisions on foreign policy. She noticed that CNN touched audiences' emotions in a way that made them react in a particular way.

(56) When the government first began regulating radio and TV broadcasts, it gave the justification that:

The correct answer is: (C) Airwaves were scarce

The government gave the excuse that there was a shortage of airwaves and hence there was a need for it to regulate broadcasts via both radio and television. When broadcasts are done, if one frequency is used by two or more channels, it becomes difficult to decipher the messages. Therefore, the government took that challenge as its reason to intervene with transmissions, to ensure each person or entity broadcasting had a frequency that would not interfere with those of other broadcasters.

(57)What does the "Fairness Doctrine" mean?

The correct answer is: (A) It is an FCC policy stating that it is compulsory for broadcasters to air all perspectives equally

This is the doctrine that demands that rival political sides get an equal amount of airtime, a doctrine right-leaning politicians disliked. This regulation was rescinded when President Ronald Reagan took office.

(58)   In a recession, the opinion of Keynesians is that the government:

The correct answer is: (A) Should increase its spending

According to Keynesians, it is preferable for the government to increase its spending when the country is undergoing a recession, as this has the effect of raising demand, albeit artificially; consequently, the economy will be stimulated while the increased demand is being met.

According to Maynard Keynes, recessions lead to high levels of unemployment, since people are not spending much. As such, the government needs to spend more money in order to stimulate spending, and it is worth doing so even if means the government is borrowing the money to spend. However, Keynes also highlighted infrastructure—roads and bridges plus other public works—as the best way through which the government should infuse money into the economy during a recession.

(59)   Which of the options below matches a renowned economist to the wrong influential work?

The correct answer is: (B) Milton Friedman – *The Return of Depression Economics*

The Return of Depression Economics does not belong to Milton Friedman. Paul Krugman, a distinguished US economist and New York columnist, wrote the piece.

(60)   There are some countries whose Gini indices are high. What is also true of those countries?

The correct answer is: (A) A lot of wealth is concentrated within a tiny section of society

The Gini Index has to do with income distribution within a population, and when it is high it means there are great income inequalities among people. It is a measure of distribution of a statistical nature, which statistician Corrado Gini created in 1912. The Gini Index is employed in gauging inequalities of an economic nature by giving measurements of income distribution or inequalities in distribution of wealth within a given population.

(61)When calculating the GDP of the United States, _____ is omitted.

The correct answer is: (C) Profit earned by a Brazil-based company whose owner is a US citizen

The profit earned by a company in Brazil cannot be part of the US GDP, even if that profit was earned by an entity owned by a US citizen. GDP stands for Gross Domestic Product, and it comprises income earned within a country's geographical borders.

However, such income would be included in the US GNP, or Gross National Product, as it is earned by a US national. In short, GDP is a measure of local productivity irrespective of the nationality of the people involved, while GNP is a measure of the productivity of a country's nationals notwithstanding where they reside and work.

(62)   At an all-you-can-eat buffet, John hungrily eats his first full plate, fills a second one and enjoys it, but then realizes that, as much as he would like to, he cannot possibly eat a third plate. Choose one option from those listed below that explains this the way an economist would.

The correct answer is: (A) The marginal utility of the food has decreased

When a person consumes food until he simply cannot eat any more, it means its marginal utility is decreasing. That means for any additional morsel of food, the value he is getting from the food is becoming less. From the example given, it is clear John is enjoying the food less with every additional plate, meaning the utility value of every additional plate of food is becoming less and less.

Generally, in the field of economics, the term "utility" is used to describe the benefit a person derives from consuming a given product. As such, a product's marginal utility is the change in that benefit as the person increases consumption of that product. The law of diminishing marginal returns states that you derive the most benefit from the very first unit you consume, and you can go on observing the benefits until the point at which with every additional unit, the benefit becomes less.

(63)   In macroeconomics, efficiency is best described as:

The correct answer is: (A) Maximizing total utility through allocation of resources

Efficiency in macroeconomics means allocating scarce resources in a way that maximizes total utility. An example of efficiency is when a product is sold to the buyer with the highest bid, giving the seller the best price for the product while the buyer who values the product most receives the product, hence maximizing utility.

(64)   Market failure is said to happen when:

The correct answer is: (C) Resources are not efficiently allocated by the market

Market failure happens when markets fail to allocate resources in an efficient manner. Such a situation can occur when monopolies, public goods, moral hazard, asymmetric information or externalities are present. For example, if a company is able to save money through polluting but another company loses business because of the pollution, then the pollution is not properly priced and this happens because of lost market value. Government regulation can be used to re-price this negative externality.

(65)   When a government prints a large amount of money, what effect does that commonly bring about?

The correct answer is: (B) Prices in this currency rise

When a government prints a large amount of money, the prices in the currency rise. This is called inflation. The printing of more money causes the real value of the currency to drop. To cover this difference, prices in the currency shoot up. The prices of the same products in a different currency are, however, not affected.

Inflation has several disadvantages. One of them is a drop in "real wages," meaning what the wages can be used for. During inflation, people can buy less than they used to before inflation using the same wages. So, even if a person's nominal wage remains unchanged but inflation sets in, the person is bound to suffer some economic loss. Another disadvantage is that any savings you had also drop in value just like the wages. This phenomenon usually hurts senior citizens the most. Inflation also puts a country at a big disadvantage, as the prices of the country's exports inevitably rise. This makes those products less competitive in the world market.

(66) Why would company X contract with company Y to produce shirts if company X does a better job both at producing the shirts and selling them compared to company Y?

The correct answer is: (D) Because of company Y's comparative advantage in producing the shirts

If producing shirts consumes a lot of time and the profit margin is low, then company X can contract with company Y to do that work as company X focuses on retail sales, which are more lucrative. Because company Y is bad at both producing shirts and retailing them, it has lower opportunity costs, and that is the company's comparative advantage.

(67) What is the equilibrium price of a product?

The correct answer is: (B) The price point where supply and demand are equal

Equilibrium price refers to the price point where supply and demand are equal. When prices go up, fewer people are able to buy the goods, and that causes a surplus. When the prices drop, the demand increases, and that causes a shortage in goods.

In normal circumstances and in a free market economy, sometimes supply exceeds demand; at other times, demand exceeds supply. When supply is higher than demand of a given product, the product is offered in the market at a lower price than when demand is higher. For example, during the potato harvesting season, a 90-kg bag of potatoes will cost much less than it will three or four months down the line. On the other hand, over the Christmas season, the same bag of potatoes is likely to cost much more.

(68) Marginal costs of manufactured goods decrease as the production volume goes up. Why does that happen?

The correct answer is: (C) Fixed cost can be spread over many more units

When there is an increase in production volume, fixed costs, like machinery and rent, are spread over more units. For example, cost per unit is lower when the fixed cost is spread over 20,000 units than when it is spread over 15,000 units.

Even if you have a processing plant meant to produce 10,000 cans of fruit per week, producing 5,000 cans in one week does not reduce the amount of space your business needs for storage. It means if you are using hired storage space for your target 10,000 cans, you will still pay the same when your actual rate of production is lower. Obviously, the unit cost of such storage drops when you have produced more units than when you have produced fewer units. Even salaries of permanent staff remain the same whether you produce more or less in a manufacturing firm. You should look at fixed costs as those costs that remain constant no matter how much you produce.

(69)   What is likely to happen when government controls prices on wheat but the cost of production of the wheat exceeds the imposed price?

The correct answer is: (B) A wheat shortage will be experienced

A wheat shortage is likely to be experienced because wheat farmers are less likely to sell their wheat to avoid losing money. Such a scenario occurred in the United States in the 1970s when the US government imposed price controls on gasoline and OPEC increased crude oil prices. Because of this, it was impossible for retailers to make more money from buying oil from OPEC than selling it, so there was a great shortage of gas.

Such scenarios make a free market preferable, because even when some suppliers raise their prices, somehow the market manages to balance itself and establish an ideal price for everyone. That's because when buyers reduce their consumption owing to rising prices, some suppliers invariably cave in and reduce their prices. Consequently, people shift to the suppliers with lower prices and the other suppliers have no choice but to follow suit.

(70)   What causes the difference between short-term and long-term effects brought about by demand change?

The correct answer is: (D) Adjusting to a market involves a certain cost

The difference between long-term and short-term effects is the cost involved when adapting to a market. For instance, a farmer who wants to know whether to grow wheat or corn will first check the prices of the seeds. However, if a farmer has already purchased the seeds, throwing them away and buying different seeds for another crop would result in a loss.

(71) Which of these statements best describes digital information?

The correct answer is: (C) Information recorded under discrete data

Digital information refers to any information recorded under discrete data. Digital data is stored using binary encoding in computers, but it can also be stored in different ways. Analog data, like recorded music on LP records, is continuous data and not discrete.

There are many advantages associated with digital systems, and one of them is the capacity to switch applications without having to change your hardware; this is called "easy programmability." Another advantage is the versatility of the systems that has led to reduced hardware expense. Because processing of digital signals is very fast, processing of data digitally is extremely fast. Digital systems are also highly reliable and making corrections is convenient because of the availability of codes for error correction. It is also easy to reproduce results. This is not the same with analog systems, in which temperature, noise and humidity are all issues to contend with.

(72)   Which of the statements below is false about the advantages of LCD monitors over CRT monitors?

The correct answer is: (B) An LCD monitor is cheaper

It is not true that an LCD monitor is cheaper than a CRT monitor. LCD monitors use less space and were invented mainly for laptops, so they do not use large monitors. LCD is an abbreviation used for a screen that has a flat panel and makes use of a liquid crystal display. Although laptops mainly used LCD screens for a time, the technology is now being extensively used for desktop computers as well as a replacement for traditional monitors that used to be very bulky and utilized cathode ray tubes.

(73)   How was the floppy disk named?

The correct answer is: (A) It got its name because of the bendable nature of the disks

Floppy disks were easily bendable, so the name "floppy disk" was coined. Later designs were more rigid, but the name did not change.

(74)   What makes random access memory (RAM) random?

The correct answer is: (C) It is not exactly random, but RAM is able to gain access to any given data point at any given time

RAM is able to gain access to any data point anytime. In the past, cassette tapes played only the currently exposed bits, while eight-track tapes could play only from the start all the way to the end.

(75) What is the role of the BIOS?

The correct answer is: (B) It is responsible for loading the OS

The basic input/output system (BIOS) is responsible for loading the operating system (OS). It turns a computer's hardware on and then runs a code known as a boot sector that boots the OS.

The term "BIOS" is used for computer instructions that control an operation's input and output.

The OS is system software with the capacity to utilize the resources of both hardware and software in providing basic services for use by different computer-based programs. Great examples of operating systems are MS Windows, Linux Operating System, Apple iOS, Apple macOS and even Android OS.

(76)   What is the importance of a central processing unit cache?

The correct answer is: (C) The absence of a cache will cause the CPU to miss many clock cycles

The absence of a cache will cause the CPU to miss many clock cycles. A CPU does not store memory of its work to perform calculations. For the CPU to carry out a calculation that requires data, it needs to wait until the data arrives. A cache holds data and helps minimize the delay. Fast CPUs require large caches in order to maximize storage.

(77) Which of the choices below describes the main limitation found in backward-compatible systems?

The correct answer is: (D) Backward-compatible systems must be highly complex

The major disadvantage found in backward-compatible systems is that they are very complex. This characteristic causes them to be less stable and more prone to hacking. Windows operating systems work to be backward-compatible while Apple does not strive for backward compatibility as much. Most Linux distributions do not strive at all to be compatible.

(78)   What does Moore's law state?

The correct answer is: (B) Every two years, processing speed doubles

According to Moore's law, processing power should double every two years. This law is based on Gordon Moore's prediction, which initially stated that there would be twice as many transistors fitting on one silicon chip every two years. Moore's prediction has continued to hold true over the last 50 years.

(79)   When you use a computer with no graphics card, what is likely to happen?

The correct answer is: (B) There will not be any images

The absence of graphics cards means that no image will appear. Today, graphics cards have diverse functions, but their main responsibility is to put images on your monitor. A graphics card is responsible for picking up the relevant signals and converting them into comprehensible data that is displayed on your computer monitor.

(80)   Which of these does not represent malware?

The correct answer is: (D) Your system being accessed by a hacker

Malware refers to any unwanted software in your system, so a hacker gaining access to your system cannot be termed malware. Some malware is harmless to your computer, a good example being adware, which is a legal type of malware.

You can also define "malware" as software designed purposely to cause disruption in your processing work or to cause damage to your work. Malware is software that gets access to your computer system without express authority to do so. Malware is aptly described as software that is "malicious."

Malware can be in the form of a virus, spyware or adware or other varied kinds of harmful software. Malware is known to slow down computers and drastically reduce the speed at which you are able to browse the internet. Malware can cause problems that make it difficult for you to connect to various networks.

Malware can be exemplified by viruses and worms, spyware and Trojan horses and others. It is highly recommended that you protect yourself from malware by installing antivirus software and other anti-malware software from credible sources.

(81) Which process below is not managed by the OS?

The correct answer is: (A) Maintaining interoperability

Maintaining interoperability is the responsibility of a software developer and not the central processing unit. The role of the OS is to manage system resources and allow interaction between applications and hardware.

The term "interoperability" can be defined as a computer system's capacity to perform exchanges of information while also making use of it. This applies to software as well. For example, some software has interoperability, meaning it can work well with devices designed by varying manufacturers.

(82)   Which of the options below is not an algorithm?

The correct answer is: (C) Software documentation

An algorithm refers to a systematic way of solving an issue. The problem can be anything from preparing a meal to cleaning a computer or operating equipment. Software documentation cannot be classified as an algorithm. The term "algorithm" can also be used to describe a step-by-step problem-solving method, and it is commonly employed in the processing of data and where massive calculations are required. Algorithms are handy when carrying out operations of a mathematical nature. They are also great at data manipulation, for example where you need to sort data in a certain order to identify a target item.

(83)   Which of these is the least complex algorithm?

The correct answer is: (A) Exhaustive search

Of the above algorithms, exhaustive search, which is also referred to as the brute-force method, is the simplest algorithm. The exhaustive search works by trying all answers to find the one that works best. This method is time-consuming, so not many problems can be solved using it. If you were to factor long primes using this method, it would take you centuries to complete the task.

(84)   Which of the statements below explains how prototyping works in the software engineering field?

The correct answer is: (B) A rough and approximate version that shows proof of concept is quickly designed

A prototype is a rough-estimated version of a program and should be designed in the very first stages. It should represent the look as well as the function of the final product. Once approved, a prototype can be improved on and refined.

(85)   Why is C considered one of the lower-level languages in programming?

The correct answer is: (B) The programmer is able to directly control hardware and memory

C is among the lower-level languages in programming because it directly interacts with hardware. The programmer is also able to control hardware and memory allocation. Because of its direct interaction with hardware, C is one of the high-performance languages.

(86)   Define an object in object-oriented programming.

The correct answer is: (A) A data field or data set and the associated methods

Objects are data structures, which include data sets as well as functions or methods for operating the data. In modern-day software engineering, the most dominantly used programming languages are object-oriented languages.

(87) Which of these describes one of the main advantages of cloud computing?

The correct answer is: (A) There is more efficient use of resources

A major advantage associated with cloud computing is the efficient use of resources. In cloud computing, virtual workspaces are connected, with each user accessing the internet from their terminal. The system's resources are allocated to each workspace dynamically, ensuring that no resources are underutilized.

(88) What is the difference between protocol and algorithm?

The correct answer is: (C) Algorithms indicate what should be done, while protocols also indicate who should do it

Protocol does not only indicate what should be done but also the person responsible for the task. For example, recipes can show you how meat should be cooked, but protocols also indicate who should buy the required ingredients, prepare the meat and other such key details.

(89) Between public key encryption and private key encryption, which is mostly used in modern encryption?

The correct answer is: (C) Both types of encryption keys are used

Both private and public key encryptions are used in modern encryption. Private key encryption is faster and more secure than public key encryption. It is, however, difficult to distribute a private key, so the majority of security protocols use a public key encryption that shares a private key and then use that private key through the remaining session.

(90) Why is JPEG format considered lossy?

The correct answer is: (B) There is a loss of data when compressing

When converting files to a JPEG format, some data gets lost. That is why JPEGs are referred to as lossy. Lossy compression helps reduce the size of a media file that does not require great resolution. There are other formats that provide lossless compression, and they are ideal when you need to maintain high definition.

(91) What dictates an Ethernet network's maximum size?

The correct answer is: (B) The collision domain

An Ethernet network's maximum size depends on the collision domain. Messages are usually sent across nodes, but sometimes receiving nodes are busy, so the message is re-sent to the node where the message was transmitted from. The time taken from when the message is sent out, bounced back from the busy receiving node and back to the transmitting node dictates the collision domain of the network. Faster networks usually have shorter collision domains.

(92) Which computer network is the internet considered to have originated from?

The correct answer is: (B) ARPANET

The internet is considered to have originated from ARPANET, a network that was created by US Department of Defense to connect research facilities and universities that had ARPA-related contracts.

(93) Which agency regulates IP addresses?

The correct answer is: (B) ICANN

ICANN is a nongovernmental organization that was formed in 1998 by the US government. Its role is to maintain IP addresses.

(94) Describe open-source software.

The correct answer is: (D) Software that has a source code that is freely available

Open-source software refers to software that has a freely available code. Since it has an open-source code, anyone is able to examine, alter or redistribute an altered version of the software program.

(95) What is a major disadvantage to relational databases?

The correct answer is: (C) The presence of redundant data

The major disadvantage of a relational database is redundant data. Redundant data consumes additional memory space in the database and it can cause inconsistencies in the system if not managed properly. You can reduce redundancy through a process known as normalization, which involves organizing relational databases.

(96) What activity is responsible for reducing a large amount of data into smaller, meaningful sets of data that can be used?

The correct answer is: (B) Data mining

Data mining refers to the process of reducing a large amount of data to make it usable information. The process mainly involves getting rid of data that is not interesting.

(97) Define re-identification in online security.

The correct answer is: (C) Using anonymous information to determine the actual identity of a user

Re-identification refers to the use of anonymous information to determine the real identity of a user. Valuable information can be sold once you have determined its origin.

(98) What does error encoding mean?

The correct answer is: (B) A type of copy prevention that creates errors intentionally to establish authenticity

Error encoding refers to a type of copy prevention that creates intentional errors to establish authenticity. A floppy disk was encoded with a bad sector and the program would look for it before running. A copying floppy disk could not transfer those bad sectors and the program did not run. This tactic is no longer used, since floppy disks have long been phased out. But there are techniques that still use a similar concept today.

(99)   Describe white-hat hackers.

The correct answer is: (C) They expose vulnerabilities in cyber security so that those vulnerabilities can be fixed

White-hat hackers bring vulnerabilities in cyber security to light so that those vulnerabilities can be looked into and corrected. In some instances, however, these activities can sometimes be controversial or illegal, as some of white-hat hackers exploit vulnerabilities for their own personal gain.

(100) Which of the options below can be a part of metadata in a document?

The correct answer is (D) All of the above

Metadata can hold all of this information. Most users are not aware of metadata, so it is a serious privacy issue.

(101) In the sentence below, which section do you think needs editing for incorrect grammar, incorrect spelling, wordiness or inappropriate choice of words?

According to her report, a ten year old girl helped the injured man by the roadside.

The correct answer is: (A) *A ten year old girl*

Compound adjectives should be hyphenated, so the phrase *ten year old* should be written as *ten-year-old*. If the sentence was written as *The girl is ten years old*, then it would not be hyphenated.

(102) What action will help improve the sentence below?

Remember to fix the leaking roof when you get home, you might get into trouble when it rains again.

The correct answer is: (C) Correct the comma fault

Correcting the comma fault will best improve the sentence. You can have a conjunction immediately after a comma or use a semicolon in place of the comma.

(103) What action will improve the sentence below?

If they would have put all their money in that bank, they would be penniless now that the bank went under.

The correct answer is: (A) Eliminating the tense shift

The sentence will flow much better when you remove the unnecessary tense shift. A possible way to fix this conditional sentence is by removing would and having your sentence read, *If they had put all their money in that bank, they would be penniless if the bank went under.*

(104) Which action will improve the sentence below?

After intense training, the girl's football team scored their first goal in two years.

The correct answer is: (C) Replace *their* with *its*

The team is a singular unit, so *its* should be used in place of *their*. When using British English, however, you can use collective nouns in plural form.

(105) Which action will best improve the sentence below?

The engine was washed before leaving the garage in case the impure oil had settled at the bottom of the engine.

The correct answer is: (B) Use active voice

You use fewer words when communicating in active voice than when using passive voice. You should use passive voice only when you want to emphasize the object in a sentence.

(106) Which action will best improve the sentence below?

Lying on the wet grass, Lisa found her lost diamond necklace.

The correct answer is: (D) Fix misplaced modifiers

You can improve the sentence by correcting misplaced modifiers. The modifier in place can be seen as describing Lisa and not the lost diamond necklace. After being corrected, the sentence will read, *Lisa found the lost diamond necklace lying on the wet grass.*

(107) Which action best improves the sentence below?

The three triplets had a lovely time at the top-notch hotel.

The correct answer is: (A) Discard *three*

It is important to avoid using unnecessary words in a sentence. We know that triplets represent three, so to avoid a wordy sentence, we can leave out *three.*

(108) Which action will improve the sentence below?

The beautiful song, that featured in the Lion King *film, was composed by Travis.*

The correct answer is: (A) Eliminate commas

The sentence will sound better when the commas are removed. You should not set off an essential clause in a sentence with commas.

(109) Which action best improves the sentence below?

The dress which I wore to the party needed to be stitched because I ran a hole through it.

The correct answer is: (C) Use *that* instead of *which*

In English, there is a rule that indicates that *which* can be used only in parenthetical remarks and it is advisable to use *that* instead.

(110)   Which action will improve the sentence below?

Torn and weary, Linda decided to buy new office chairs.

The correct answer is: (C) Place the modifier in the right position

When you read the sentence above, it sounds as though Linda is torn and weary because the modifier has been misplaced. When you change your sentence, it will read, *Since her office chairs were torn and weary, Linda decided that it was the right time to purchase new chairs.*

(111)   Which of the actions below will best improve this sentence?

He couldn't get to see the skit because he had a task to complete.

The correct answer is: (D) Use *could not see* instead of *couldn't get to see*

Using *could not see* instead of *couldn't get to see* makes the sentence easier to read.

(112)   Which action will improve the sentence below?

There was a large amount of tourists visiting the Preston Museum on a daily basis.

The correct answer is: (A) Replace amount with number

The sentence sounds better when you use *number* instead of *amount*. We use *amount* when referring to uncountable quantities, such as milk or water. People are countable, so the correct word to use is *number*.

(113)   Which action will best improve the sentence below?

Despite his seemingly generous nature, his deeds were, at the end of the day, self-indulgent.

The correct answer is: (C) Get rid of the hyphen in *self-indulgent*

You can use a hyphen on compound adjectives only when the phrase or noun to be modified comes after that compound adjective. If the compound adjective comes after the modified phrase or noun then a hyphen should not be used.

(114)   How can you define liquidity trap?

The correct answer is: (D) When individuals with disposable income refuse to invest as they await a drop in prices

It is said there is a liquidity trap in the economy when people who would otherwise invest refrain from doing so, as they anticipate a decrease in prices. What such people may not realize is that their anticipating a drop in prices and subsequent refraining from investing is the real reason the prices end up dropping. In short, if a significant number of people with cash stop buying things or investing, it results in reduced demand, and when demand drops as supply remains constant, prices are ordinarily bound to drop.

Even with a problem of liquidity, it does not help to inject cash into the economic system. As long as in the minds of potential investors there is a chance they will spend less than today if they refrain from investing a little longer, they will continue causing a decrease in demand.

(115)   How is stagflation best explained?

The correct answer is: (A) An economy that is not only stagnant but also has escalating inflation

When the term "stagflation" is used to describe the state of the economy, it means there are two negative elements affecting the economy, namely a high rate of inflation and stagnation. For the economy to do well, it should not be stagnating. This means a lot of economic activity should be going on, with money frequently changing hands.

There was a time when economists assumed there was no correlation between recessions and inflation, believing them to be mutually exclusive. This was believed to be true until there was stagflation in several countries in the 1960s and 1970s.

(116)   What is the government's way of measuring inflation?

The correct answer is: (C) It assesses the changing value of a wide range of values

To measure inflation, the government takes a wide range of values and monitors how those values continue to change. It particularly focuses on products that people are likely to purchase, observing how many of those products they are able to purchase and how much they spend on them at any one time. The samples taken serve to show people's way of spending the money they have.

(117)   Is it possible to have per capita income go up as median income goes down?

The correct answer is: (B) Yes, and it signifies increasing inequality

It is correct to assume inequality is increasing whenever per capita income rises while the median income drops. This can be seen in the following example.

There are 10 people with an annual income of $100,000. For some reason, nine of those people find their salaries slashed by half, and they now earn $50,000 each per year. In the meantime, the salary for the remaining person increased tenfold so that it is now $1,000,000 per year. What was the per capita income before and what was the median salary?

"Per capita" means the average income one person earns within a given locality within a set period of time. It is calculated by adding everyone's income and dividing it by the number of people in that locality, or its population. In this case, the population is 10 people and the total income is $1,000,000. The initial per capita income, therefore, was $1,000,000 ÷ 10 = $100,000.

As for median income, it is that amount dividing the affected income distribution into two equal parts: the income that falls right in the middle after all individual incomes are arranged either in descending or ascending order. In this case, the median was initially $100,000. In short, the per capita and the median incomes were equal.

After the changes in salaries, now the per capita income is:

$(1,000,000 + (50,000 x 9)) ÷ 10, which is $(1,000,000 + 450,000) ÷ 10

$(1,000,000 + 450,000) ÷ 10 = $1,450,000 ÷ 10

$1,450,000 ÷ 10 = $145,000.

As for the new median, it is $50,000, as 9 out of 10 people earn $50,000.

In short, the per capital income has risen from $100,000 to $145,000 while the median has drastically dropped from $100,000 to $50,000.

(118)   A factory has been producing 1,000 units of a product, but now management has decided to produce 1,001 units of that same product. What best describes the cost of producing the extra unit?

The correct answer is: (C) The marginal cost

Any time you are engaged in production, the cost you incur to produce a single extra unit is referred to as marginal cost (MC). Correspondingly, the revenue you earn by adding just one unit extra is referred to as marginal revenue (MR). If you find that you are earning higher marginal revenue than the amount of marginal cost you are incurring, you can conclude it makes economic sense to add an extra unit to your production. Another term used in the same context of marginal cost and revenue is "equilibrium." To attain equilibrium in production, you produce your units until marginal cost is equal to marginal revenue, or MC = MR.

(119)   Select the action that correctly modifies the following statement:

Windstorms are an "every day" occurrence in most of the Northwest United States.

The correct answer is (C) Rewrite *every day* as *everyday*

Everyday is the right word to use since it is an adjective and modifies the occurrence. *Every day*, on the other hand, is a noun that is modified by an adjective.

(120)   Select the action that correctly modifies the following statement:

Joe Thomas is one of the NFL quarterbacks who has won more than one Super Bowl.

The correct answer is (C): Replace *has* with *have*

The statement is correctly modified when *has* is replaced with *have*. Joe Thomas is part of a collective team—the quarterbacks who have won several Super Bowls.

(121)   Select the action that correctly modifies the following statement:

She was honest, hardworking and a regular customer at the nearby pub.

The correct answer is (D): Correct the parallel structure

The statement is improved when the parallel structure is corrected by changing all the three descriptions to nouns. In the current structure, the first and second descriptions are adjectival, whereas the third description is a noun. An example of correct structure is: *She was a hardworking employee, an honest lady and a frequent client at the nearby pub.*

(122)   Select the action that correctly modifies the following statement:

The current senator was scared of not retaining his seat; he used a no-holes-barred method during the campaign.

The correct answer is (C): Replace *no-holes-barred* with *no-holds-barred*

No-holds-barred is a wrestling phrase that refers to a brutal method of wrestling that allows all forms of holding, including methods that may cause severe injury or lead to death.

(123)   Select the action that correctly modifies the following statement:

When the Johnsons's family car was broken into, the radio was stolen and the window broken.

The correct answer is (A): Replace *Johnsons's* with *Johnsons'*

When *Johnsons's* is replaced with *Johnsons'*, the statement will be correctly modified and follow the plural possessive rule. Many people confuse plural possessives by adding an extra *s* at the end of the word, which is not needed.

(124) Select the action that correctly modifies the following statement:

Despite not being able to buy the brand-new Cadillac, Chris was able to go on a test drive with the Cadillac after convincing the dealer to allow him.

The correct answer is: (B) Replace *test drive* with *test-drive*

The term *test drive* is not appropriate because if the verbs composed of two words are left together, it means that one verb modifies the other, which is not appropriate. To correctly modify the statement, introduce a hyphen between the two words. Thus, the correct term is *test-drive*.

(125) Select the action that correctly modifies the following statement:

Completing a marathon is an impressive fete regardless of how long it takes.

The correct answer is (D): Replace *fete* with *feat*. A *fete* refers to a festival, whereas a *feat* refers to an achievement.

(126) Select the action that correctly modifies the following statement:

The Republican Party has particularly strong supporters in the southern state.

The correct answer is: (B) Uppercase *southern*

The statement is improved when *Southern* begins with a capital letter. This is because *southern* in this statement specifically refers to a region. However, when referring to a direction, the word is lowercased.

(127) Select the action that correctly modifies the following statement:

After canceling the appointment at the last moment, he felt badly, but he didn't have enough time to make it at the expected time.

The correct answer is: (A) Replace *badly* with *bad*

Badly as an adverb is used to imply doing a job poorly. However, in this case it is supposed to mean negative emotions and, therefore, the correct word is *bad* and not *badly*.

(128) Select the action that correctly modifies the following statement:

The streets were frozen over, the paths were extremely slippery.

The correct answer is (C): Correct the comma splice

It is incorrect to join two independent clauses using a comma. So we need to replace the comma with a semicolon or conjunction.

(129) Select the action that correctly modifies the following statement:

The new CEO of the company had large future plans, but the board was adverse to changing too quickly.

The correct answer is (C): Replace *adverse* with *averse*

The statement is improved when *adverse* is replaced with *averse*. *Adverse* refers to something detrimental to a person's best interests, whereas *averse* refers to something that you do not agree with. With regards to the statement given, the board did not support the idea of change. Hence they were averse to and not adverse to.

(130) Select the action that correctly modifies the following statement:

Whoever will be selected for the scholarship will be entitled to four years of full tuition.

The correct answer is (A): Replace *whoever* with *whomever*

The statement will be correctly modified when *whoever* is replaced with *whomever*. This is because the statement is in passive voice. Therefore, the selected person acts as the object of the statement and not the subject.

(131) Select the action that correctly modifies the following statement:

A group of people have demanded an end to the US boycott on Cuban goods.

The correct answer is (D): Replace *boycott* with *embargo*

The statement is correctly modified by replacing *boycott* with *embargo*. Despite the two words both referring to trade, they have different meanings. *Boycott* is used when consumers decide not to purchase certain products, and *embargo* refers to when the government decides to impose a law preventing consumption of certain products from a particular country.

(132) Select the action that correctly modifies the following statement:

Neither party was completely satisfied with the judgment made by the mediator, but they nonetheless complied.

The correct answer is (A): Replace *mediator* with *arbitrator*

The statement will be correctly modified if *mediator* is replaced with *arbitrator*. The difference between the two is that, whereas a mediator is in charge of the negotiation process, he does not have the power to impose a decision on the parties. However, an arbitrator takes the place of a judge and, therefore, has the power and responsibility to determine the final results of a negotiation.

(133) Select the action that correctly modifies the following statement:

The daughters requested that their father take a break from his work and accompany them to the mall so that they could meet some of they're friends.

The correct answer is (C): Replace *they're* with *their*

The statement is correctly modified when we replace *they're* with *their*. *They're* is a short form of *they are* and is not appropriate in this statement structure. However, *their* is a third-person plural possessive pronoun.

(134) Select the action that correctly modifies the following statement:

After spending three hours in traffic to get to the trendy restaurant, John intended to stay for awhile.

The correct answer is (B) Eliminate *for*

The appropriate action is to eliminate *for*. Considering the fact we have used *awhile*, which represents a short time, using *for* is considered repetitive. Another option is to split *awhile* into *a while* and retain *for*.

(135) Select the action that correctly modifies the following statement:

Due to HR bureaucracy, it had become impossible to establish whose responsible for late paychecks.

The correct answer is (D): Replace *whose* with *who was*

The correct way to modify the statement is to replace *whose* with *who was*. *Whose* is a possessive pronoun and cannot be used in the given sentence. On the other hand, *who was responsible* is the correct phrase to be used in the given sentence.

(136) Select the action that correctly modifies the following statement:

The moment it was discovered that the hedge fund carried out some dirty deals, the SEC dispatched an auditor to pour over the company books.

The correct answer is (A): Replace *pour* with *pore*

Pour is generally associated with liquids. *Pore* refers to the process of examining something in detail, such as when one is curious to determine the tricks used in accounting.

(137) Select the action that correctly modifies the following statement:

The audience was tricked into believing that the hero had died towards the end of the film.

The correct answer is (B): Replace *towards* with *toward*

Most formal writing prefers the use of *toward* more than *towards*.

(138) Select the action that correctly modifies the following statement:

The board of directors are still pondering over whether to release more bonds. Nonetheless, the company still needs more liquidity.

The correct answer is (D): Replace *are* with *is*

The statement's subject, *the board of directors*, is singular. Therefore, *are*, which, is plural, should be replaced with *is*, which is singular.

(139) Select the action that correctly modifies the following statement:

The rule of law, a middle class that is developing and free elections are all crucial to a vibrant, functional democracy.

The correct answer is (D): Correct the parallel statement

In order to modify the statement correctly, it is important to correct the parallel structure. *The rule of law, a developing middle class and free elections* is a correct parallel structure.

(140) Select the action that correctly modifies the following statement:

Some parts of the country continue to operate without daylight savings time.

The correct answer is (B): Replace *savings* with *saving*

The correct word to use is *saving* and not *savings*. However, it is common to see *daylight saving time* wrongly expressed as *daylight savings time*.

(141) Select the action that correctly modifies the following statement:

The board constitutes eleven individuals from departments across the company committee.

The correct answer is (B): Replace *constitutes* with *comprises*

The statement is correctly modified when *constitutes* is replaced with *comprises*. *To comprise* refers to what something is made up of. Therefore, eleven individuals can constitute a board, but a board cannot constitute the individuals.

(142) Select the action that correctly modifies the following statement:

The novel affected great personal growth in my years as a teenager, so I've recommended it to various teens ever since.

The correct answer is (D): Replace *affected* with *effected*

Affect is a verb meaning *to alter*, whereas *effect* is a verb meaning *to bring about*. According to the statement, the novel brought about great personal growth in the writer. Therefore, the appropriate word to use is *effect*. Hence the statement should be, *The novel effected great personal growth in my years as a teenager.*

(143) Select the action that correctly modifies the following statement:

As soon as the closed-door meeting came to an end, there were off-the-cuff remarks inferring I would be passed over for promotion.

The correct answer is (C): Replace *inferring* with *implying*

Infer refers to reaching a conclusion with limited detail, whereas *imply* means suggesting something without explicitly saying it. Therefore, the correct action in this statement is to replace *inferring* with *implying*.

(144) Select the action that correctly modifies the following statement:

After going through both copies, the English professor concluded that the rough draft was the best copy.

The correct answer is (B): Replace *best* with *better*

Best is a superlative of three comparisons, so it is inappropriate in this case. However, since the comparison the professor is making is between two copies, the correct word to use is *better*.

(145) Which region in China has the largest population?

The correct answer is (D): Eastern region of China

The majority of the Chinese population resides in the country's eastern region. The main reason for this is the soil's rich fertility and the close proximity to the ocean.

(146)   In which world region is Latin America located?

The correct answer is (B): To the south of the United States in the Western Hemisphere

Latin America is the entire region to the south of the United States and within the Western Hemisphere. The areas under this region were colonies of Portugal and Spain, which is why their main languages are Spanish and Portuguese.

(147)   Name the geographic feature with the largest impact on Polish history.

The correct answer is (A): The location of the Great European Plain

The location of the Great European Plain had a very great impact on Polish history. It was the easiest route from Asia to all of Europe, and most soldiers frequently passed through Poland.

(148)   When is a country said to be doubly landlocked?

The correct answer is (D): When that country and its neighbors are all landlocked

For a country to be doubly landlocked, both the country and its neighbors have to be landlocked. Two well-known doubly landlocked countries are Uzbekistan and Liechtenstein.

(149)   A topological map can best be used for:

The correct answer is (D) Identifying mountain height

Topological maps are common for determining relative height and are designed to indicate terrains. Therefore, they are the right maps for establishing a mountain's height.

(150) What has been the result of the Sahara Desert on Africa's development?

The correct answer is: (C) It led to separate development of the northern regions of Africa and sub-Saharan Africa

Due to its harsh, dry condition, the Sahara Desert was not often crossed by traders and other individuals. Consequently, the sub-Saharan Africa and Northern African regions have developed independently, separate from the rest of Africa.

(151) Why are the Suez Canal and the Strait of Gibraltar important?

The correct answer is (B): They facilitate the Mediterranean trade

The Suez Canal and the Strait of Gibraltar are both very important, as they control the trade routes within the Mediterranean region. The Strait of Gibraltar is still under British control.

(152) Why did Russia try to conquer Turkey in the 1800s?

The correct answer is (D): Russia wanted a warm-water port

The main reason Russia attacked Turkey with so much zeal was that it wanted to secure trade during winter. Russia wanted a warm-water port to compensate for its ports, which freeze in winter. A port is said to be warm-water if it is able to retain its liquid state even during winter.

(153) Name the geographical feature that played a major role in China's development.

The correct answer is (A): The north and west mountain ranges

The mountain ranges in the north and the west of China contributed to the isolation of the country's development. This was the case with the desert on the western side and the oceans on the southern and eastern sides, although China actually had access to its neighbors.

(154) Name the geographic element that was a contributing factor to isolationism in America.

The correct answer is (A): The oceans located in the west and east

The fact that the west and east of America were bordered by ocean left it with only two neighboring nations—to the north and to the south. Due to this, America was left out of most world affairs.

(155) In which period were modern European towns developed?

The correct answer is (B): The Middle Ages

The increased level of commerce and trade in the Middle Ages contributed greatly toward the development of the modern European towns. It was during this period that current businesses, such as banks, began.

(156) What was the most notable long-term effect of the Crusades?

The correct answer is (B): The demand for goods from the East

Crusaders brought luxury items, such as spices, thus increasing trade in the East.

(157) What element contributed to the flourishing of the Renaissance in the northern part of Italy?

The correct answer is (D): The wealthy elite that supported artwork

The wealthy elite that provided great support for art acted as a contributing factor to the Renaissance in northern Italy. One of the families commonly known for its great support for art was the de' Medici family.

(158) Select the ethical system that is closely parallel to Bushido, the code of conduct that the Japanese samurai adhered to.

The correct answer is (B): Medieval chivalry

Both Bushido and medieval chivalry acted as codes of honor and were greatly followed by feudal society warriors.

(159) Which of the following is vital for industrialization?

The correct answer is (A): Food surplus

Food surplus is a key factor for industrialization. A food surplus reduces the number of people needed to engage in agriculture because there is already sufficient food. That labor force can then venture into industrial activities, thus promoting industrialization. The major point here is that it is difficult, if not impossible, to succeed in industrialization when people hardly have enough to eat.

(160) What was the social category that obtained great power in 1789 following the French Revolution?

The correct answer is (D): The middle class

During the French Revolution in 1789, the middle class, also known as bourgeoisie, obtained a lot of power. The new constitution granted them great political influence and increased power.

(161) Which of the following resulted from Stalin's agricultural collectivization program?

The correct answer is (B): Food shortages

Stalin's collectivization program caused terrible food shortages. During the Soviet command of the economy, the production of food was organized in various quotas, enough to feed the entire Russian population. However, the quotas were not met regularly, and that caused a food shortage.

(162) Which of the following did not at all contribute to the development of WWI?

The correct answer is (A): Religious violence

The main factors behind World War I included imperialism, nationalism, alliances and militarism. Religious differences were not considered a contributing factor.

(163) Which event compelled the emperor of Japan to describe himself as "only human"?

The correct answer is (D): The loss of World War II

After losing World War II, the emperor of Japan declared himself "only human." He used this phrase when he declared his surrender so that future leadership would not be affected by his decisions.

(164) What novel provision did the United States insist be part of the new Japanese constitution after World War II?

The correct answer is (A): A reduction in Japanese military size

The Japanese military has always been very small compared to the country's size. After World War II, the United States stressed the importance of Japan agreeing to reduce its military size even further and required that this be included in the new Japanese constitution.

(165) What characteristic was common in both Communist Russia and Nazi Germany before World War II?

The correct answer is (A): One-party government in control

Both Nazi Germany and Communist Russia had the same one-party rule despite the political differences within their systems. The two communities were both totalitarian, and the views of the people not in power were not considered to be important.

(166) What was Gorbachev's policy in the 1980s?

The correct answer is (C): Glasnost

Gorbachev's policy of openness was known as Glasnost. Gorbachev hoped that government transparency would play a key role in the elimination of the corruption that was ruining the Soviet government.

(167) Which nation does not regard itself as communist?

The correct answer is (B): North Korea

Despite not describing itself as a communist country, North Korea is described as being communist by most media. Other countries with communist parties include Cyprus and Nepal.

(168) Which of the following happened next after the Roman Empire fell?

The correct answer is (D): Weak central government and general mayhem

After the fall of the Roman Empire, a hundred years of mayhem and feudal societies followed.

(169) In which city did Aristotle, Socrates and Plato teach philosophy?

The correct answer is (C): Athens

Ancient Athens is known for its great contributions to mathematics, philosophy, arts and theatre. It was in Athens that Socrates, Plato and Aristotle taught philosophy.

(170) Name the nation that was once ruled by the Mamluks, Fatimids and Ayyubids.

The correct answer is (B): Egypt

The Ottoman Empire ruled ancient Egypt, Istanbul and Damascus. The Mamluks, Fatimids and Ayyubids ruled Egypt during the era of the Ottoman Empire. Egypt's independence came as a result of the country's strong political system and its distance from the other regions under the Ottoman rule.

(171)   What differentiates Andalusia from the rest of Spain?

The correct answer is (A): It was ruled under Islamic law for about 700 years

The Andalusia region of Spain was under Islamic law for about 700 years. The name Andalusia is Arabic for "Al-Andalus," meaning 'The land of vandals." In 1492, the Moors were driven out of southern Spain, thus liberating the region.

(172)   Name the first European to locate North America.

The correct answer is (B): Leif Ericson

Five hundred years before Christopher Columbus went to North America, Leif Ericson traveled to North America and settled there temporarily before returning to Greenland.

(173)   What was the primary goal of the African National Congress during apartheid?

The correct answer is (A): Establish the one-person one-vote system

During the apartheid regime in South Africa, only white people were allowed to vote. Consequently, the primary role of the African National Congress was to ensure that each person was entitled to one vote.

(174)   What factor do Kemal Ataturk and Gamal Nasser have in common?

The correct answer is (D): Neither had a strong relationship with the West

Both leaders were focused on creating modern nations and centralizing power in their regions.

(175)   According to the US Constitution, which government branch is supreme?

The correct answer is (D): None

By giving separate power to the three government branches, the Constitution allowed each branch to have power over the remaining two, thus allowing a check-and-balance system. Therefore, none of the branches is deemed more powerful than the others.

(176)   George Washington was a member of the _____ political party.

The correct answer is (D): He was not in any political party

George Washington was the only American president without a political party. He was opposed to the idea of political parties.

(177)   What is the function of the Department of the Interior?

The correct answer is (B): Management of US natural resources and heritage sites

Whereas in most countries the department of the interior is responsible for intelligence gathering and internal security, the Department of the Interior in the United States is assigned the duty of managing natural resources and heritage sites such as the national parks.

(178)   What is the department assigned to manage US borders?

The correct answer is (C): Department of Homeland Security

The Department of Homeland Security is assigned the duty of ensuring safety along the US borders. Despite there being other agencies responsible for such security, the Department of Homeland Security cuts across all jurisdictional boundaries.

(179)   What is the US military branch that does not report back to the Secretary of Defense?

The correct answer is (C): The Coast Guard

Despite being considered a branch of the US military, the Coast Guard commandant reports to the Homeland Security secretary. The Coast Guard commandant is not a member of the Joint Chief of Staff.

(180) The top rank in the US Army is:

The correct answer is (A): General of Armies

General of Armies is the topmost rank in the US Army, despite having been held only two times. The first to hold the rank was John Pershing in 1919 after World War I. Later, George Washington was posthumously awarded the title in 1976 during the bicentennial. Ordinarily, the top rank in the army is general of the Army.

(181) What one factor does not guarantee US citizenship?

The correct answer is (B): Having one parent who is a US citizen

Having one parent a US citizen does not guarantee the child US citizenship. For the child to be a citizen, the parent would need to have lived in the United States at least five years.

(182) Massachusetts, Virginia, Kentucky and Pennsylvania are all commonwealth states. What is their legal difference from the other 46 states?

The correct answer is (A): There is no legal difference

The fact that these four states are known as commonwealth states emphasizes that their governments are established through popular will. But being a commonwealth state has no constitutional effect, so these states are no different from the other 46.

(183) What organization does not belong to the US government?

The correct answer is (B): The World Bank

The World Bank is not a US government organization. It is composed of 147 member countries. However, the United States is the largest shareholder, which explains why World Bank presidents have always been citizens of the United States.

(184) What is a controversial method used by a president to dismiss a bill without directly vetoing it?

The correct answer is (B): Pocket veto

This is a method of dismissing a bill indirectly. When a bill is sent and received by the president, the president has 10 days to sign it into law or reject it. However, if the president takes 10 days before signing the bill into law, it automatically becomes a law. Nonetheless, the congressional session might end before the 10 days. In such a case, the bill is automatically rejected because it was not vetoed. Congress will then have to start the bill ratification process again from scratch.

(185) A blueprint has a line whose length is 1.5 yards. In the blueprint, one yard represents 0.9 meters. Roughly how long is that line in terms of meters?

The correct answer is: (B) 1.35 meters

If 1 yard represents 0.9 meters, 1.5 yards represent (1.5 x 0.9) meters.

This works out to 1.35 meters.

(186) Snacks sold in Country X last year raised revenue totaling $12 billion, made up of 34% from potato chips, 17% from tortilla chips, 13% from nuts, 13% from popcorn, 12% from pretzels and 11% from other snacks. From this information, calculate the ratio of potato chip revenue to tortilla chip revenue.

The correct answer is: (A) 2:1

To get the correct ratio, you must determine the revenue received from the sale of potato and tortilla chips. To do this, it is important to first find the total revenue earned from all the snacks. The reason is that the percentage revenues have been provided in relation to the total revenue earned.

Calculating revenue from potato chips:

Total revenue = $12 billion

Percentage that is potato chips = 34%

Revenue from potato chips = 34% of $12 billion, which is $4.08 billion

Calculating revenue from tortilla chips:

Percentage that is tortilla chips = 17%

Revenue from tortilla chips = 17% of $12 billion, which is $2.04 billion

In fact, you could simply reason that since 17% is half of 34%, the revenue from tortilla chips must be half of the revenue from potato chips, which is:

$4.08 billion ÷ 2 = $2.04 billion.

Now you can calculate the ratio:

$4.08: $2.04, which is simply 2:1

Alternatively, you could simply deduce that since the percentage revenues of the two items are in the ratio 2:1, from 34% and 17%, the actual revenue should be in a similar ratio of 2:1.

(187) Snacks sold in Country X last year raised revenue totaling $12 billion, made up of 34% from potato chips, 17% from tortilla chips, 13% from nuts; 13% from popcorn, 12% from pretzels and 11% from other snacks. Thirty percent of the revenue received from the sale of potato chips specifically came from the sale of barbecue potato chips. This means the amount of revenue that came from the sale of barbecue potato chips was:

The correct answer is: (A) $1.2 billion

The amount of revenue earned from the sale of potato chips was 34% of $12 billion, and 30% of that came from the barbecue potato chips. To find out the amount of revenue from barbecue potato chips, the calculations would look like this:

Revenue from barbecue potato chips = 30% of (34% of $12 billion)

30% of (34% of $12 billion) means 30% x $4.08 billion

30% x $4.08 billion = $1.224 billion, which can be rounded down to $1.2 billion.

(188) Lauren's earnings are $8.40 every hour, and the rate of overtime equals one and a half times the regular hourly rate. Overtime is any time Lauren exceeds 40 hours of work. If she works 45 hours in a week, what should her total pay be?

The correct answer is: (C) $399

Pay for 40 hours can be calculated as follows:

40 x $8.40 = $336

Overtime hours = 45 hrs – 40 hrs = 5 hrs

Overtime pay = 5 hrs @ $(8.40 x 1.5)

5 hrs x $(8.40 x 1.5) = 5 hrs @ $12.60

5 hrs @ $12.60 = $63

Pay for regular hours + Pay for overtime = $336 + $63 = $399

(189) Jane's shadow is 5 feet long while her father's shadow is 8 feet long. Jane's father is 6 feet tall. What is Jane's height?

The correct answer is: (D) 3 ft 9 in

The best way to go about finding Jane's height is to use the ratio of her father's height to his shadow, because both are known. Then you can proceed to use that ratio to calculate Jane's height.

Height of father = 6 ft

Length of father's shadow = 8 ft

Ratio of height to shadow = 6:8, which can be simplified as 3:4

Using this ratio to calculate Jane's height:

3/4 x 5 ft =15/4 ft = 3.75 ft

Since the answer is given in feet and inches, you can begin by setting the 3 ft aside, and then converting 0.75 of a foot to inches.

75/100 x 12 in = 9 in

The correct answer is, therefore, 3 ft 9 in.

Alternatively, you could convert feet into inches as soon as you get the correct ratio. In this case, instead of calculating 3/4 x 5 ft, you would calculate 3/4 of (5 ft x 12), because one foot equals 12 inches.

3/4 of (5 ft x 12) =3/4 of 60 in, which is effectively 3/4 x 60

3/4 x 60 = 3 x 15 = 45 in

To convert 45 into feet and inches you need to divide by 12.

45 in ÷ 12 = 3 ft (because 3 x 12 = 36) and 9in (because 45 − 36 = 9)

(190) Amit donates 4/13ths of his January paycheck to charity. In absolute figures, the amount he donates is $26.80. Calculate Amit's January paycheck in full.

The correct answer is: (C) $87.10

The best way to find the size of Amit's January paycheck is by first calculating the amount one part of 13 represents in dollars.

If 4/13 (meaning 4 parts of 13) = $26.80, 1/13 (or one part of 13) should be $26.80 ÷ 4

$26.80 ÷ 4 = $6.70

Now that you know that one part of 13 = $6.70, you can calculate what 13 parts represent by multiplying $6.70 x 13.

$6.70 x 13 = $87.10

If you want to ascertain that your answer is correct, calculate 4/13 of $87.10 and see if you get $26.80.

(191)   Given that x = 2, calculate x + x(xx)

The correct answer is: (A) 10

Substitute 2 for x, so that you now have 2 + 2(22)

2 + 2(22) = 2 + 2(4), which is the same as 2 + 8

2 + 8 = 10; so 10 is the value of x + x(xx)

(192)   Mr. Kamau sold two pipes, each at $1.20. From one pipe he made a profit of 20% based on the cost of the pipe, whereas from the other he made a loss of 20% also based on the cost of the pipe. From this information, choose the answer option that is correct.

The correct answer is: (D) Overall, Mr. Kamau lost 10 cents

1 pipe sold at $1.20 results to mark up of 20%

Let the cost of the pipe be X.

This means that X+20%X = $1.20

This is the same as saying 120%X = $1.20. So what is X?

If 120%X = $1.20,

X = $1.20 ÷ 120% or $1.20 x 100/120

$1.20 x 100/120 = $120/120, which is $1

This means that based on the cost of the pipe, which was $1, Mr. Kamau made a profit of $1.20 – $1, which is $0.20.

The other pipe was sold at $1.20.

Let the cost of the pipe be X.

Since the pipe was sold at a loss of 20%, it means that:

X – 20%X = $1.20

If 80%X = $1.20, what is X?

X = $1.20 ÷ 80% or $1.20 x 100/80

$1.20 x 100/80 = $120/80, which is $1.50

This essentially means that based on the cost of the pipe, which was $1.50, Mr. Kamau made a loss of $1.20 – $1.50, which is $0.30.

The profit from the first pipe of $0.20 plus the loss from the second pipe of $0.30 leads to a net loss of $(0.2 – 0.3), which is -$0.10.

It is important to note that the fact that the profit is based on the cost of the pipe means you need to calculate the markup as opposed to the margin.

(193) Jacques arrived in Paris by flight from Tokyo and exchanged his 50,000 yen for the equivalent francs (F). Considering a single US dollar was equivalent to 140 yen and was also equivalent to 6 francs, what is roughly the amount of francs that Jacques received?

The correct answer is: (C) 2,143 F

Begin by converting the 50,000 yen to dollars, which means calculating:

50,000 ÷ 140 = $357.14

Next convert the dollars into francs by calculating:

$357.14 x 6 = 2,142.86 F, which is approximately 2,143 F.

(194) If the rate at which Tom's savings account earns interest is 2 1/4% annually, what is the amount of interest he is expected to have earned by the end of the fifth consecutive year if he maintains a deposit of $1,000?

The correct answer is: (C) $112.50

When choosing the formula to calculate total interest earnings, it is important to note that the interest is being earned on the deposit alone and not on the interest earning in preceding year(s). Hence the formula is:

p x r x t = I, where p is the principal sum or deposit, r is the rate of interest in decimal form and t is the duration the deposit has remained earning interest.

In this case, p = $1,000, r = 0.0225 and t = 5. Hence, p x r x t will result in:

$1,000 x 0.0225 x 5 = $112.50.

(195) Which of the following is not required for a perfect market?

The correct answer is: (D) No regulation

A perfect market can still exist even when there is market regulation. In short, non-existence is not a condition for a perfect market. If you cite no existing regulation as a condition, then you are likely to be referring to a free market, which is different from a perfect market. For a market to be referred to as "perfect" there needs to be perfect competition.

Both the customers and the sellers have all the information they need to do good business, and they have equal access to technology. There are other conditions that can be associated with a perfect market, including there being no barriers, and all of them point to everything being the best for both customers and sellers. As for regulation, the only time it can be deemed to interfere with a perfect market, thus making it imperfect, is when it gives one side—buyers versus sellers—an advantage over the other.

(196) Which of the following does not exemplify insider trading?

The correct answer is: (D) Someone reads information about the organization from a newspaper and does business with the organization the same week

Options (A), (B) and (C) all exemplify insider trading. As long as someone uses information that is not in the public domain to take advantage of doing business with the organization, it is insider trading. Sometimes insider trading is done by people who work within the organization, and they take advantage of the information they have access to for their own business success. Other times such people leak confidential information to outsiders, giving those outsiders an undue advantage over other investors.

If, for example, a director in a company knows there is a scandal brewing about the CEO and that if the information reaches the media it is likely to mar the image of the company and make the share prices drop, sharing such information with a friend who is a big shareholder at the company would be insider trading. Armed with this information, this investor is likely to instantly offload his shares into the market at the prevailing prices to avoid a loss in case the share prices fall. There is regulation against insider trading, and people have been sued and jailed for it.

(197) If a company has full control of its product's life cycle from the beginning of production or sourcing of raw materials to selling the product, the term used is:

The correct answer is: (A) Vertical integration

Vertical integration describes a scenario in which an organization controls all segments of the life cycle of a given product. Vertical integration has two major benefits, one of them being that it is the organization that gets to add value to the product at every stage of the product's production process. This means it is the organization that benefits from the value added to the product because it translates to higher value of the company assets, even if it is through work-in-progress.

The other major benefit is the organization has the chance to minimize production costs just by virtue of having all necessary operations integrated.

(198)   All of the activities listed below are legal in the United States apart from:

The correct answer is: (C) Activities of a monopolistic nature

When an organization is engaged in activities of a monopolistic nature, it means it does things that ensure no other organization is able to enter the same market. By restricting entry into the market, the organization is barring fair competition and depriving consumers of choice.

Monopolies are illegal, and that makes option (C) the appropriate answer. As for the other options provided, they are all legal market strategies to help the organization gain a competitive edge in the market. When competing companies try, for example, to bring their costs of production and delivery down to afford lower prices to customers, their strategy is good for both the business and the customers.

With lower product prices, demand rises and the organization reaps greater profits. On the contrary, an organization with monopolistic practices normally does not work toward reducing prices. It strives to drive every competitor out of the market so that it can retain its high prices and still have customers buy a product because those customers have no other choice. In short, monopolies manipulate the market in a manner that is bad not only for other businesses and customers, but also for the economy in general.

There are some industries that are difficult to penetrate due to the large and costly infrastructure required. Good examples are water supply, generation of electricity and rail transport. In order to protect water, electricity and rail consumers from the negative effects of monopolies, especially because demand is pretty inelastic, these industries are regulated.

(199)   Which of the economic systems listed below is run with an underlying assumption that a nation's wealth is dependent on the country's total capital?

The correct answer is: (C) Bullionism

This economic system considers money and precious metal, such as gold, as the only wealth a nation has, which means the nation discounts other property as wealth. Bullionism is close to the mercantile system. The main difference between mercantilism and bullionism is that the latter puts emphasis on money circulation and maintenance of a positive trade surplus. A country practicing bullionism is inclined to subsidize its exports while taxing any imports.

(200) What is arbitrage?

The correct answer is: (A) Earning profits when you manipulate a discrepancy in different markets

When you notice a discrepancy or discrepancies in different segments of the market or in different markets, then you take advantage of such discrepancies, what you are doing is referred to as "arbitrage." A good example is when you find one supplier selling a bag of fresh fruits at $10, and then you realize a grocery store is buying the same bag of fruits at $20. So you decide to buy bags of fresh fruits from the seller with a low price to sell to the store owner willing to part with double the amount of money. In this case you would be making $10 for a bag of fresh fruits, which is 100% profit.

It is important to realize that arbitrage is always temporary. As more and more people begin to take advantage of arbitrage, there is an oversupply at the store, With the demand remaining constant, the store owner will naturally take fruits from the person who opts to reduce the price. With time, the market creates its own equilibrium.

CPSIA information can be obtained
at www.ICGtesting.com
Printed in the USA
LVHW011400031020
667505LV00004B/29

9 781989 726174